Office 2013

Improving Skills for the Workforce

PDTC LLC - Levietta D. Hayes

www.xulonpress.com

About Professional Development Training Center (PDTC) LLC

P DTC would like to extend a sincere thanks to the Advisory Board members, testers, and proofers for your contribution for making this book a success. Thanks to God for your sincere dedication and generous support.

The CEO of PDTC LLC has taught Information Technology courses on the Secondary and Post-Secondary levels. She has helped to train and prepare students for academic and non-academic careers as well as help adults transition in their careers through Adult Continuing Education courses.

She has worked with area local businesses to assist students to achieve goals through internship and pilot programs.

PDTC's mission is to help improve performance. Our goal is to make an effective difference in the life of others that will equip and empower them to excel.

System Requirements

Operating System Requirements: Windows 8.0 or 8.1, Windows 7, Windows Server 2008 R2, Windows Server 2012, Mac OS X 10.6 or later, Android KitKat 4.4[5]

Hard Disk Space Required: 3.0 GB available

Processor Required: 1 (GHz) or faster x86 or 64-bit processor with SSE2 instruction set

Memory Required: 1 GB Ram (32 bit); 2 GB Ram (64 bit)

Required Display: Graphics hardware acceleration requirements are DirectX 10 graphics card and 1024 x 576 resolution

Required: .Net Version: 3.5, 4.0, or 4.5

Multi-touch: Note that new touch features are optimized for use with Windows 8. A touch-enabled device is required for any multi-touch functionality. Note: all features and functionalities are accessible by an input device including a mouse or keyboard.

Additional Requirements: Systems functionality may vary based on the system configuration.

Microsoft account is required.

Professional Development Training Center LLC (PDTC)

Preface

About this book

This book provides a hands-on approach to learning that includes:

- Step-by-step instructional foundation

- Progressive advancement of higher level skills and problem solving

- Relevant exercises to improve workforce knowledge, skills and abilities

- Knowledge Check and Skill Assessment Exercises for Content Reinforcement

Student Resources

Exercise files can be downloaded from: www.pdtconline.com/

Acknowledgments

My sincere thanks to Joyce Wright and Kimberly Jackson for their valuable insight. Your prayers and support is greatly appreciated and will not go unrewarded. May God richly bless you!

To my children, Sophia, Lionel, and Benjamin, (BJ), thank you so very much for your generous support and encouragement. May God bless you greatly! Thanks to my parents, Levi Duberry and Ernestine Greene, for your love and support. Thanks to Sis Carletha Davis for your prayers and Rodney and Najia Sanders for your kindness. To my sister, Gwendolyn Greene, thanks; you have a heart of gold! And to Harriet Baxter, thanks for your prayers and encouragement! Thanks to Ganaris Smith, for your love and support!

Thanks to everyone that contributed to the success of this book. Most importantly, I thank God, the Father, Son and Holy Spirit! Blessings to all that use this book. May you be richly blessed, in Jesus name! "With men this is impossible, but with God all things are possible".

This book is dedicated in loving memory of Buena K. Wilson and Pearl Jones,
your presence is greatly missed, but your spirit lives on forever!

Contents

Purchasing Office 2013

To understand the power of Microsoft Office 2013, you must first understand that it is really a transitional change from the norm of what was! Technology is changing rapidly, and Office 2013 is an example of this movement.

The new Office 2013 has features that allow you options to work from any mobile device and the ability to sync files and documents for free with online storage known as OneDrive. Microsoft offers a free online version, known as Web Apps that include Word, Excel, PowerPoint, and OneNote. In order to use this service you must have Internet connection as well as a Microsoft account. The online version of Office, previously known as Office Web Apps has limited editing features for the applications. Office 2013 gives you several options for using the service.

- Office 2013—Traditional Desktop Version
- Office 365—The Subscription Version
- Office Online—Free with Microsoft Account

With your Office 365 subscription, you will need to set up and maintain an account. The subscription version gives you up to five different installation options to share with other family members.

My Account

In order to save and share files online, you will need to have a Microsoft account. You will need to have an email address and password to create and access a Microsoft account. See Figure 1.

There are several benefits to having a Microsoft account such as:

- Editing files in your browser

- Accessing your files from anywhere

- Sharing files online

Figure 1   Microsoft Account

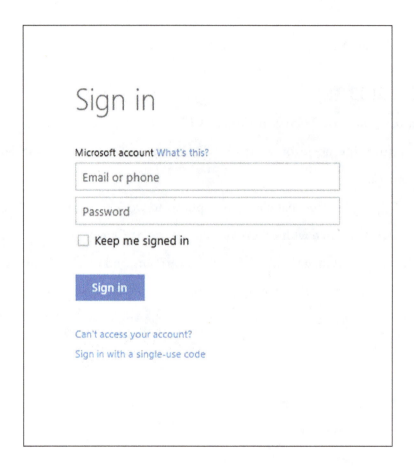

Office 365

Office 365 is the anywhere access application allowing you to stay connected from any device in this mobile world. Whether you are working remotely, from your tablet, phone etc., Office 365 gives you access to your office applications to check email, arrange conference meetings, collaborate and share documents from any location. OneDrive allows you to sync files while you are away from home, and work and have access to files online or offline.

Windows 10 was released in July of 2015. Windows 10 is available as a free upgrade to Windows 7 and Windows 8 users until August of 2016. Windows 10 promises to be the best windows ever! It is fast, secure and more compatible than previous versions.

The **Start Menu** is back and improved for quicker navigation. Windows 10 has several new amazing features. Two very popular features include:

- **Cortana** your personal digital assistant.
- Microsoft Edge provides a better web experience

Exploring Windows 8

The Interface Windows 8 is a transition from how we have interacted with computers and technology in the past. Technology has changed how we do business from day to day, and your experience with Windows 8 will continue the trend of progressive improvement.

There are several changes with the new Windows 8 as opposed to what we are accustomed. Some of **Windows 8** changes include the **start menu**, the **interface** changes, **online** features, and **improved security** features.

The **Start Screen** is totally different. It is where your **Apps** are located. Apps are placed in squares called **tiles**. See Figure 2. Some tiles are referred to as live tiles. The start screen can be personalized with changes to the color scheme, personalizing your background image, and rearranging the tile display.

Figure 2   Apps

The **Charms bar** is where you gain access to the computer settings, as shown in Figure 3. The charms bar can be accessed from swiping in from the left on your laptop or hovering in from the top right or bottom right of your computer.

Figure 3   **Charms Bar**

Live tiles are the live streams of updated information given by an App; examples would be sports, weather, travel, news, and many others. **Live tiles** can be turned on or off on your computer.

Hot corners is a new feature that lets you hover your mouse over any of the four corners of your computer to access shortcuts to other apps or return to other open pages. See Figure 4.

Figure 4   **Hot Corners**

Navigating Windows 8

The **Desktop** a familiar feature from previous versions of **Windows** with the exception being the removal of the **Start menu**.

The **Charms bar** gives you access to features like search, share, start screen, devices, and settings.

Search is used to find files and apps. See Figure 5.

Figure 5   **Search**

The **Share** feature lets you share photos and pictures through other apps, as shown in Figure 6.

Figure 6   **Share**

Start—is where you view the **apps** tile and access programs. View Figure 7.

Figure 7   Start

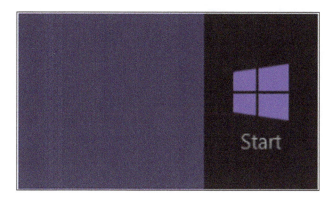

In **Apps**, right click an app to see more options.

Open apps by clicking the desired app.

Close apps by clicking the **X** on the apps title bar, as shown below in Figure 8. **Hint**: moving the mouse towards the top of the screen reveals the auto-hide features of the title bar. Or You may close an app by right clicking it from the hot-corners preview.

Figure 8   Close Apps

Devices—displays the computer hardware. See Figure 9.

Figure 9   **Devices**

Settings gives access to features like Notifications, PC settings, Control Panel, Power and more, as shown in Figure 10.

Figure 10   Settings

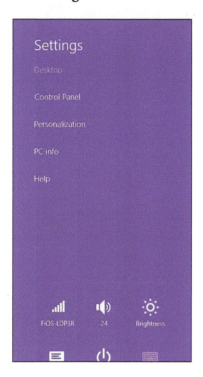

Windows 8.1

The Windows 8.1 Update and Windows RT 8.1 Update include the improvements to make Windows more familiar and convenient for devices that use touch and mouse input and to make Windows available on a wider variety of devices. The Windows 8.1 Update and Windows RT 8.1 Update also include security and performance updates. These Updates must be installed for your PC to receive any future security updates for Windows 8.1 or Windows RT 8.1.

Maintaining Files in Windows 8

File Explorer—has replaced Windows Explorer. **File explorer** helps you manage your files, search for files and folders, and view and organize files and folders. See Figure 11.

Folder views—changes how folders and files are displayed.

1. Click the view tab.

2. Choose preference from the layout group.

Figure 11   File Explorer

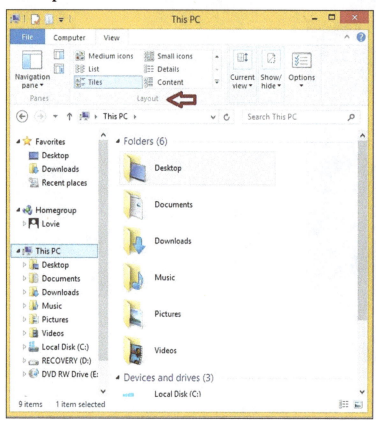

Sorting files and folders are most beneficial when you are searching for a specific file or folder or arranging files or folders in a specific order. It helps to locate files faster. There are several ways to arrange the sorting such as dates or subject. Click the **current view** downward pointing arrow to view, **sort by** choices.

Searching helps to locate files and folders. Enter the keyword in the search bar.

Create folders in several ways. To use the **File Explorer** folder.

1. Select the **new folder** tab on the **Quick Access Toolbar** of the **File Explorer** window, as shown in Figure 12

Figure 12   New Folder

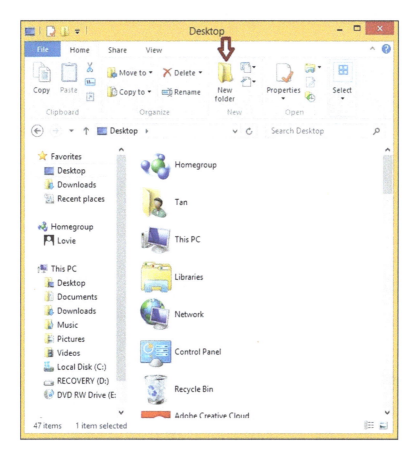

Delete files by right clicking the file or folder and selecting **delete** from the drop-down menu. **Restore files** that you deleted from the **Recycle Bin.**

1. From the **File Explorer,**
2. Select the **recycle bin** from the left pane.
3. Locate the desired file and click **restore the selected items,** as shown in Figure 13**.**
4. File will be restored to its original file location.

Figure 13   Recycle Bin

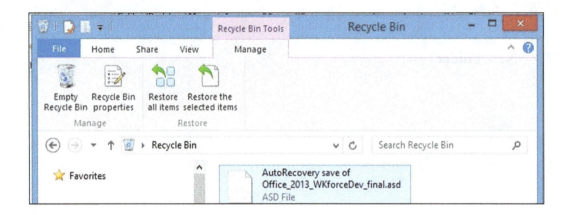

Copy files by right clicking on the file and selecting **copy** from the drop-down menu.

Renaming files/folders by right clicking the file or folder and selecting **rename** from the sub-menu that appears.

Moving files is taking a file or folder from one location to another.

1.   Right click the file or folder.

2.   Select the **cut** command.

3.   Select the desired location to move the file or folder and right click again.

4.   Paste the folder in the new location.

Internet Explorer—locate the **Internet Explorer** apps, click to open. Or go to charms search and type *Internet explorer* into the search bar.

Internet Explorer, or IE, is the default web browser for Windows 8. While there are two versions of IE in Windows 8, this lesson will focus on the desktop version of Internet Explorer not the start screen version as shown in Figure 14.

Figure 14   Internet Explorer App

Navigating Websites

Address bar—type an address in the Uniform Resource Locator (URL) bar and press enter from the keyboard to navigate to a website. See Figure 15.

Figure 15   Address Bar

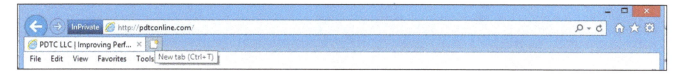

Search for information by putting in keywords in the address bar. The search engine will return a list of suggestions to choose from.

Favorites—add websites to your list to visit at a later time.

1. Click the **favorites** tab on the **IE** toolbar.

2. Select **add to favorites**, **add a favorite** dialog box opens, as shown in Figure 16.

3. Click **add.**

4. Website will be added to your **favorites** list.

Figure 16   Add Favorite

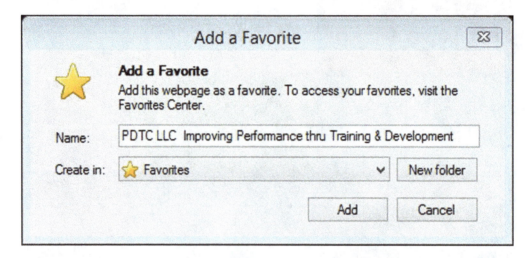

5. **Add new window** by clicking the new tab button. (This will open a new browser window).

6. **Close IE** by clicking the X in the right corner of the website window.

Word 2013

Word is a software processing tool that allows you to create, edit, and print documents. Some documents may include business letters, resumes, flyers, and brochures. Many businesses use Word as a tool for communicating with their customers.

This tutorial will help you to improve your skills, knowledge, and abilities with the Word application. Lessons are designed to guide you through the essentials and then introduce you to some advanced concepts that are relevant to the workforce.

Word 2013

Section I   Word Essentials

W1.1 Open a Blank Document

1. To open **Word,** tap or click the start screen button in the lower left corner of the screen.

2. From the start screen, begin typing "**Word**." (The search panel will open).

3. Select the **Blank document. A new** document will open.

Figure 1.1   Open Blank Document

W1.2   Word Graphical User Interface—(GUI)

In order to interact with the common tasks in Word you would need to become familiar with the interface shown below in Figure 1.2. View **Word** and identify the basic features.

Compare and contrast the screen in Figure 1.2 with your screen.

Refer to Table 1.1 for Description of Word Features.

Figure 1.2   Word GUI

Table 1.1   GUI Word Features and Descriptions

Indicator	Features	Description
1	Ribbon	Tabs are on top. Groups are on bottom and commands are in between.
2	Quick Access Toolbar	Common tasks button
3	Title Bar	Shows name of document and application name.
4	Zoom Indicator	Zooms in or out of document.
5	Document views	Document viewing adjustment
6	Status bar	Displays document information (pages, word count. Right click the status bar to customize it.
7	Help Feature	Provides resources such as videos, tutorials, and online assistance.
8	Minimize button	Minimize the screen
9	Restore button	Restores the screen
10	Vertical scroll	Used to view parts of a document (up/down).
11	Horizontal ruler	Used to manually set the margin

W1.3   Exploring the Ribbon

The Ribbon is designed with **Tab** buttons on top (Home, Insert, Design . . .) and **Group** associated buttons (Clipboard, Font, Paragraph . . .) on the bottom. These commands allow you access to **Word's** common tasks as shown in Figure 1.3. There is also an option to view or hide the ribbon depending on your preferences, see Figure 1.4.

The **file** tab also referred to as, "**backstage view**" is where you access the Word **Options** panel along with many other features such as printing, saving, and exporting.

Note: Contextual Tabs are also displayed on the ribbon. However, **contextual tabs** only appear when an object is selected to give further command options for working with that particular object

Figure 1.3   Ribbon

Figure 1.4   Show/Hide Ribbon

To customize the tabs on the Ribbon:

1. Select the **file** tab as shown below in Figure 1.5.for backstage viewing.

2. Click **Options** from the navigation pane on the left.

3. Click the **Customize Ribbon** command from the categories on the left.

4. On the right, (under **customize ribbon**), click **new tab** (at the bottom of the dialog box) as shown in Figure 1.6.

    ❖ **Note:** the new tab and new group appears together as a set.

5. Make sure **new tab** is selected then click **rename**. (Enter a name for the new tab).

6. Next, select **new group** and click the **rename** tab to give the new group a name of your choice, (a **rename** dialog box will open with an *option* to choose an image).

7. With your new group selected, choose your group associated commands, (these are the commands that you use regularly such as the font, font size, the format painter, paste . . .).

8. Select your commands from the choices on the left and **add** them to your new group on the right.

9. Click **OK** when finished.

Figure 1.5   File Tab (Backstage)

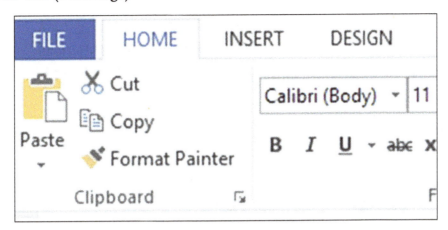

Figure 1.6   Customize Ribbon

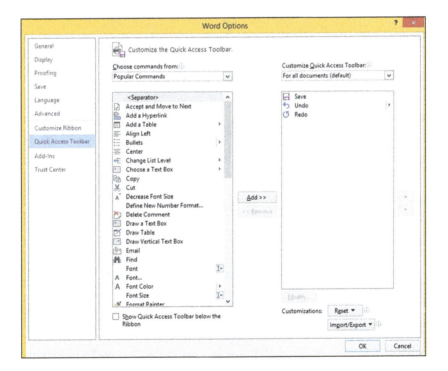

W1.4   Customizing the Quick Access Toolbar

The Quick Access Toolbar allows you to add commands that are accessed regularly. The Quick Access Toolbar is located either above or below the ribbon.

1. In order to access the **Quick Access Toolbar**, select the drop-down arrow to the right of the Access Toolbar depending on the location, as shown in Figure 1.7.

2. Select the command that you wish to add.

❖ **Note**: In order to choose more commands, click the "**more commands**" option to add more items to your Quick Access Toolbar.

Figure 1.7   Quick Access Toolbar

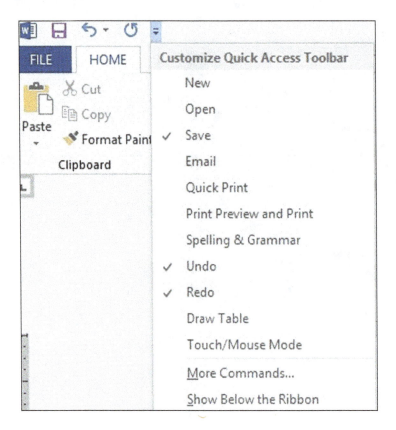

W1.5 Word Help Feature

The **help** feature displays information on Word. Click the question mark [?] located in the top corner of the screen. Enter a word or phrase to search, and a list of topics will be displayed.

You can also access this feature by pressing **F1** on your keyboard.

Section 2   Creating a Word Document

   I.   Open a New Word Document

   II.   Open an Existing Word Document

   III.   Working with Word Templates

   IV.   Inserting Text into a Word Document

   V.   Saving a Word Document

   VI.   Page Layout and Word Printing Options

   VII. Closing/Exiting Word

Student Resource Folder Word_2

W2.1 Open a New Word Document

1. Select the **File** tab.

2. Select **New**, then click **Blank Document. (A Blank Document** will open).

W2.2 Open an Existing Document

Documents that were previously saved to your computer, OneDrive, or flash drive can be accessed for modification. To locate existing files:

1. Click the **File** tab.

2. Select **Open** from the navigation pane on the left, as shown in Figure 2.1.

3. Click **Computer;** then **browse** to locate the existing document. (Select your existing document from the open dialog box).

   ❖ **Note:** Browse the **Recent Documents** to search for files that were recently opened instead of browsing through your computer files.

4. Click **Open** at the bottom of the dialog box. See Figure 2.2.

Figure 2.1   Open an Existing Document

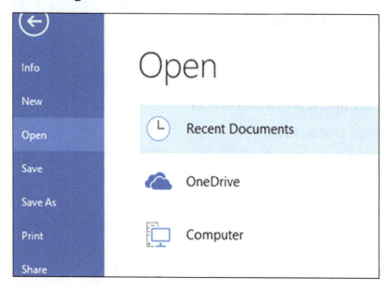

Figure 2.2   Open Document

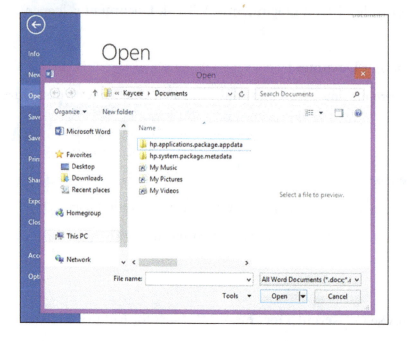

W2.3 Working with Word Templates

Predesigned documents are called **templates.** Templates have customized designs and formatting to save you time. To access **Word** templates.

1. Click **File**.

2. Next, click **New**. (The panel of **Templates** will appear).

3. Choose a **Template** to preview, then click **create** to download your desired template. See Figure 2.3.

Figure 2.3   Selecting predesigned template

W2.4 Inserting Text into a Word Document

1. Open the **BusinessLetter** document located in the Student Resource Folder.

2. Select the placeholder text, by *triple clicking* the **[Return Address]** and enter **Student's Name and current mailing address.**

3. Next, enter the **current date.**

4. Select the placeholder text **[Inside Address]** and enter the company address as follows: **800 S. Boulevard Suite 337, South Palm Beach, CA 91007.**

5. Select the placeholder text **[Salutation]** and type *Dear Ms. Sophia June:*

6. Complete the last two paragraphs of the **Business Letter** with the information from Table 2.1.

Table 2.1   Business Letter

> ❖ I would very much welcome the opportunity to discuss in detail my professional skills and talents that I possess. I look forward to discussing why I should be considered as your Instructional Systems Developer.
>
> ❖ My resume is attached for your review. I can be reached at 555-705-1122. I look forward to hearing from you concerning the Instructional System Developer position.

7. Next, click the placeholder text **[Closing]** and type *Sincerely,*

8. Select the current name and replace it with your first and last name.

9. Select the placeholder text **[Enclosures]** and replace it with **Resume attached.**

10. **Save** the document.

W2.5 Saving a Word Document

When documents are created, you will need to save it initially in order to be able to retrieve it later. Word offers two options for saving documents: The **Save** and **Save As** options.

Save As: This option should be used to initially save a Word document. This option can also be used to make a copy of an original document or rename a document.

1. With the **BusinessLetter** document open to save.

2. Click the **file** tab.

3. Select **Save As**, click **computer** then **browse**, as shown in Figure 2.4.

4. From the **Save As** dialog box, choose the desired location to store the document, (Word_resource_files).

5. Name the document **MyBusinessLetter.**

6. **Save** document.

Figure 2.4   Click File to Save a document

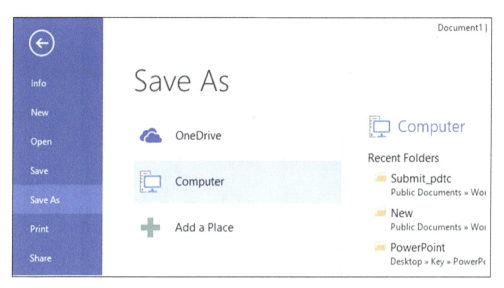

Note: Documents can be saved and stored to the local computer or to other multimedia devices, such as a flash drive, external drive, or Microsoft's online Cloud storage.

W2.6 Page Layout and Word Printing Options

In order to print a Word document in **Portrait** or **Landscape**.

1. Open **MyBusinessLetter.**
2. Click the **Page Layout** tab and select the down arrow, (as shown in Figure 2.5) for the **Orientation** command in the **Page Setup** group.
3. From the drop-down menu, choose either (**Portrait or Landscape**) to change the document's **Page Orientation**.
4. Continue.

Figure 2.5   Page Layout

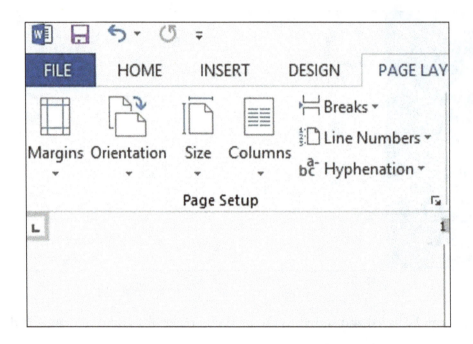

W2.6.1   Checking Page Margins

Margins add the finishing touches to your document. The margin includes the blank space from the edge of the text in the document outward to the edge of the page.

1. With **MyBusinessLetter** still open,

2. Click the **Page Layout** tab; choose the **Margins** command in the **Page Setup** group.

3. Select the down arrow, as shown in Figure 2.6.

4. Choose from the selection. (Margins will adjust immediately).

5. Continue.

Figure 2.6   Checking Page Margins

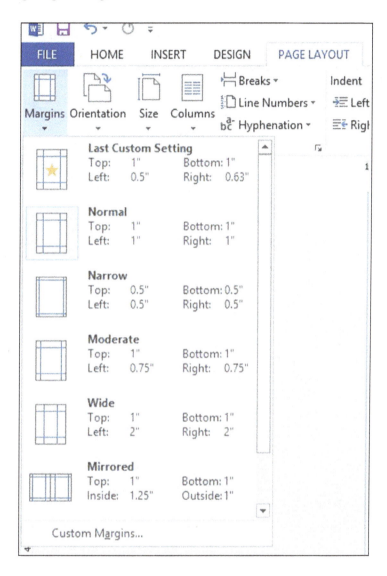

For Customized Margins

1. Select **Custom Margins** from the drop-down menu to view the **Page Setup** dialog box, as shown in Figure 2.7.

2. Make margin adjustments. Click **OK** when finished. (Margins will automatically adjust to the new settings).

Figure 2.7   Customizing Page Margins

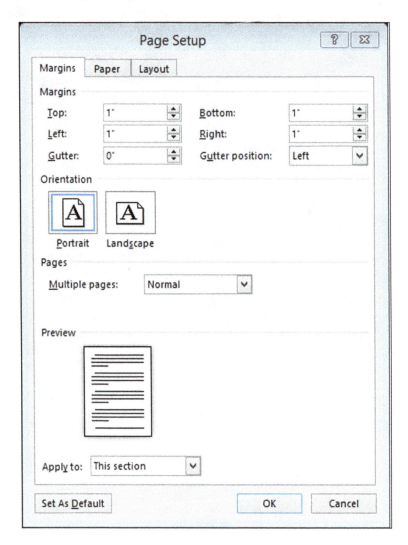

W2.6.2   Checking Paper Size

By default, paper size in **Word** is set to **Letter** size, which is approximately 8.5 by 11 inches.

1. Continue with **MyBusinessLetter.**
2. Click the **Page Layout** tab, select the **size** command in the **Page Setup** group.
3. Click the down arrow to choose a paper size, as shown in Figure 2.8. (Changes will show immediately).

Figure 2.8   Adjusting Paper Size

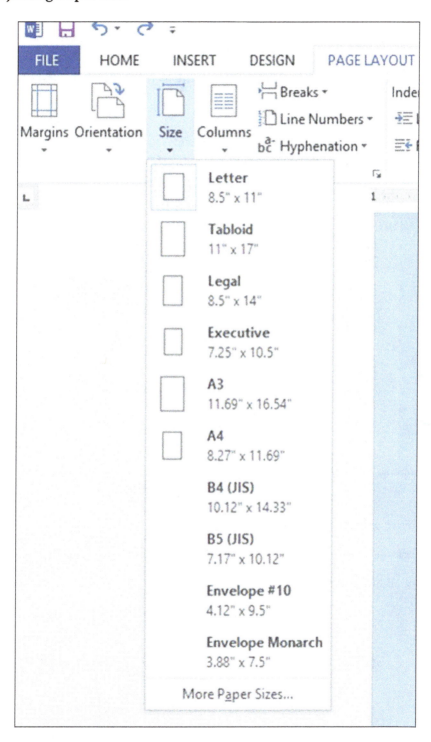

W2.6.3   Word Printing Options

After previewing a document for margin adjustments and proofing, it is then ready for printing. Previewing and Printing a document can be done from the same window, as shown below in Figure 2.9.

1. With **MyBusinessLetter** still open,

2. Select the **File** tab.

3. Select the **Print** command from the navigation on the left.

4. **Preview** the document in the **preview** window pane to the right of the screen.

5. **Print** when ready.

6. **Continue** to close.

Figure 2.9   Print Preview a Word Document

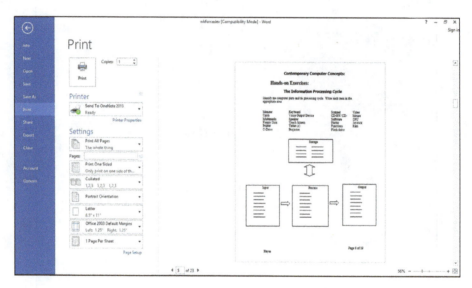

W2.7   Closing/Exiting a Word Document

To close Word, click the **File** tab and choose the **close** command from the navigation pane, as shown in Figure 2.10. Make sure all files are saved before closing.

Figure 2.10   Closing a Word Document

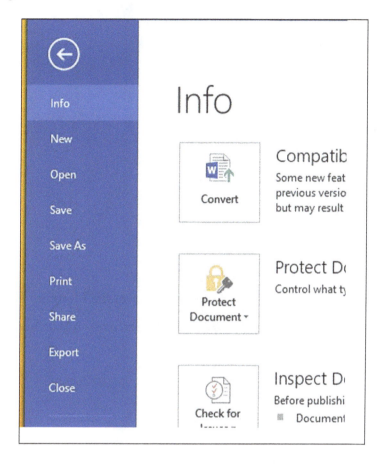

Exiting the Application

Exiting the document closes the application. **Word** will prompt you to **save** any changes to the document before **closing** and **exiting** the application. You may also **exit** Word by clicking the X in the upper right hand corner of the screen.

Section 3   Modify a Word Document

   I.   **Selecting/Deleting Text**

   II. **Copy, Cut and Paste**

   IV. **Finding/Replacing Text**

   V. **Formatting Text**

   VI. **Headers/Footers**

   VII. **Spell Check**

[Student Resource Folder Word_3]

W3.1 Selecting Text in a Word Document

1. Open the **Protocol** document.

2. Left click your mouse, hold and drag over the text to select the **Domain Types,** as shown in Figure 3.1. (**Note:** This should all be done simultaneously). Selected text will be **highlighted**. Release mouse once text is selected.

Figure 3.1   Selected Text

Domain Types:	
Type	**Description**
.biz	business
.com	commercial
.edu	educational
.gov	U.S. government
.int	International organizations
.mil	U.S. Department of Defense
.name	Personal
.net	Networks
.org	Nonprofit organizations

W3.1.2   Deleting Text in a Word Document

Deleting text removes it from the desired location in the document. Ways to delete text can be accomplished by the following:

1. Open the **Thanks** document.

2. Select item 4 in Paragraph 3, (**Restate your match**) click **delete** from the keyboard.

   ❖ You may also place the insertion point to the left of the text to be deleted and depress the delete key on the keyboard.

   ❖ Clicking the backspace button also allows you to delete text to the left of the insertion point.

W3.2 Copying and Pasting Text in a Word Document

There are times that you may want to copy text from one part of a document and paste it into another part.

1. With the **Thanks** document still open.

2. Select **Thank the Employer** from Paragraph III, item 2.

3. Click the **Copy** command located on the **Home** tab of the clipboard group, (this creates a copy of the selected text and places it on the **Clipboard** for later use) as shown in Figure 3.2.

   ❖ **Note**: You may also use shortcut keys such as: CTRL+C for copy, and CTRL+V for paste.

Figure 3.2   Copy Command

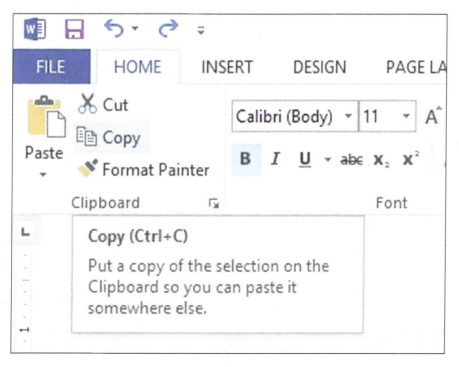

4. Place the insertion point at the beginning of Paragraph I, item 1, then click the **Paste** command located on the **Home** tab of the **Clipboard** group to insert the desired text.

W3.2.1   Cut and Paste Text in a Word Document

Cutting text removes the text from the desired location and places it on the clipboard, making it available for later use.

1. Select **Briefly** in Paragraph III, item 2; now select the **Cut** command located on the **Home** tab of the **Clipboard** group, as shown in Figure 3.3.
2. Place the insertion point in front of the comma (**,**) in Paragraph II, item 2.
3. Click the **Paste** command.
4. **Save** and continue to the next section.

Figure 3.3   Cut Command

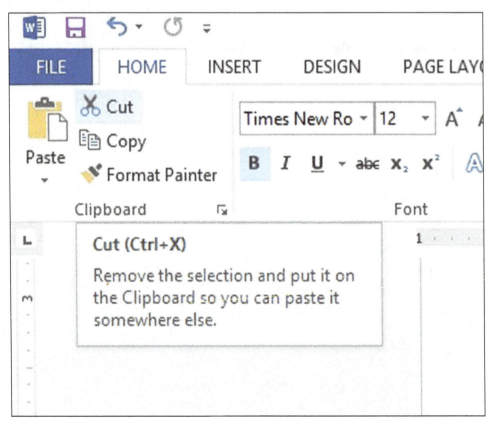

W3.3 Finding and Replacing Text in a Word Document

To search for specific words in a document, Word features the **Find** command.

1. With the **Thanks** document still open,

2. On the **Home** tab in the **Editing** group, select the **Find** command, as shown in Figure 3.4.

3. Type *Tell* in the navigation field, as shown in Figure 3.5

4. Once the desired text is found, a preview of the text will be highlighted.

5. Use the up/down arrows to step through and view each instance of the word in the document. (To exit the **Find** navigation pane, click the **X).**

6. **Continue** to next section.

Figure 3.4   Find/Replace Text

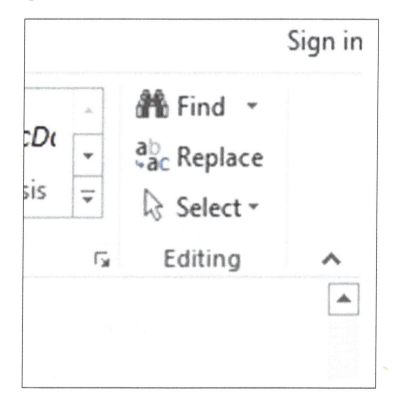

Figure 3.5   "Find" Navigation Pane

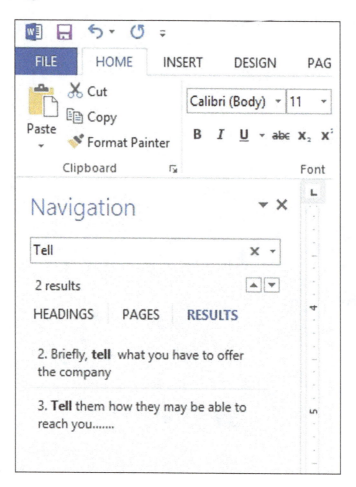

W3.3.1   Replacing Text in a Word Document

After you have used the **Find** command to search for specific text in the document, you may discover that you would like to **replace** it with another word of choice**.**

1. From the **Home** tab of the **Editing** group, select the **Replace** command. A **Find and Replace** dialog box will open.

2. Type *Provide* in the **replace with** field, as shown in Figure 3.6.

3. Click **Replace** and the selected text will be replaced.

4. Click **X** to close the dialog box.

5. **Save** and **close** the document.

Figure 3.6   Find and Replace Dialog Box

W3.4 Formatting Text in a Word Document

Formatting text consist of changing the look or appearance of your document. Formatting will help bring emphasis to certain words or phrases in the document. There are many ways to format text, some of which include changing the font, font size, font color, or font alignment.

Word has a feature called **Format Painter**, and it will copy the formatting of a selection and apply it to another area of the document. Format painter works like a brush. Once you like the look of a specific phrase or text, select it and click the format painter to copy the formatting, then brush the new selection to apply the formatting.

In this section we will modify the text alignment.

1. Open the **Webpages** document.
2. Select the **Creating Web Pages** title and select the **align center** command from the **Home** tab in the **paragraph** group, as shown in Figure 3.7.
3. **Save** and continue.

Figure 3.7   Align Center

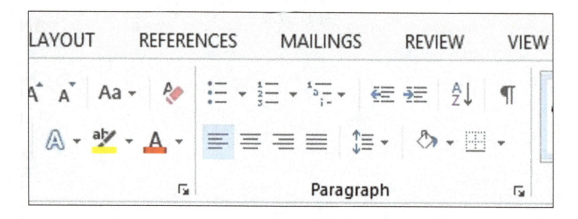

W3.4.1   Changing the Font and Font Size

1. With **Webpages** still selected.

2. Select the bulleted text and click the drop-down arrow of the **Font** command in the **font** group of the **Home** tab. Change the Font to **Verdana**, as shown in Figure 3.8.

3. With the bulleted text still selected, click the drop-down arrow for the **font size** and change the font size to **12,** as shown in Figure 3.9.

4. With the bulleted items still selected, click the **Format Painter** (to copy formatting).

5. Next, brush the non-bulleted item(s) under the heading, **(Access)** to apply the same formatting.

6. Repeat step 4 and 5 for the heading, (PowerPoint).

7. **Save** work and continue.

Figure 3.8   Font Window

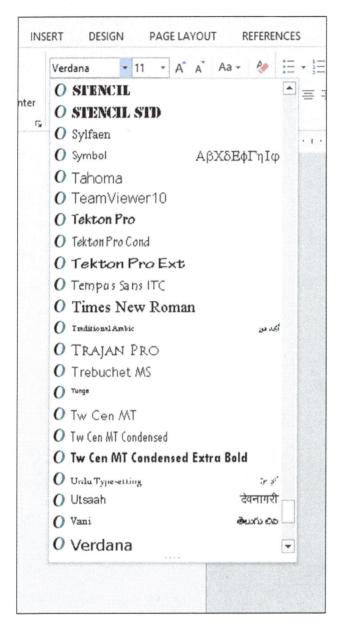

Figure 3.9   Font Size Pane

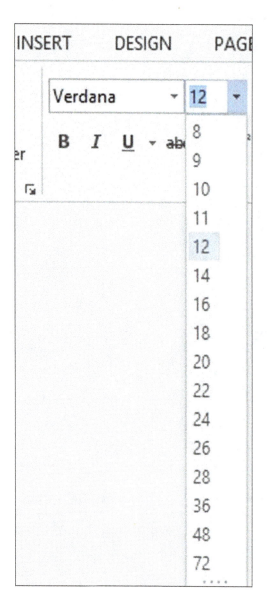

W3.4.2   Changing the Font Color

1. With **Webpages still** open,

2. Select the bulleted text (for Excel) and click the drop-down arrow for the **Font color**, on the **home** tab. (A color palate will appear, as shown in Figure 3.10).

3. Change the **font** color to **blue**.

4. Use the Format Painter to copy the formatting to the remaining bulleted items in the document.

5. **Save** and close.

Figure 3.10   Font Color Palate

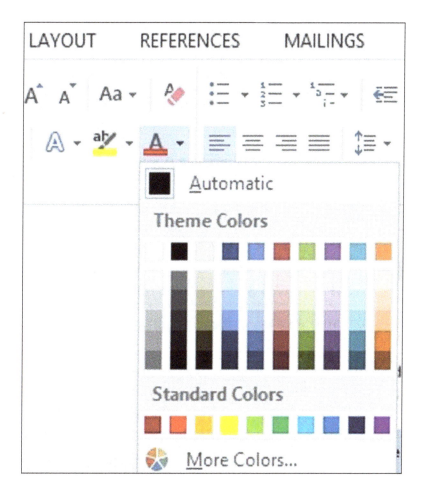

(**Hint:** other text formatting options in Word would include: **Bold (B)**, Italic (*I*), Underline (*U*)).

W3.5 Headers/Footers

A header and footer is added to a document to add important information such as: (page numbering, dates, document references, as well as other information). Word includes many preset headers.

1. Open the **Protocol** document.
2. Click the **Insert** tab and select the **Header** drop-down arrow in the **Header & Footer** group.
3. Choose **Austin** from the preset header selection, as shown in Figure 3.11.
4. Type [*Your name*] in the header.
5. Click X to close **Header/Footer** tools contextual tab, as shown in Figure 3.12.
6. **Save** and continue.

Figure 3.11   Header/ Footer Selection

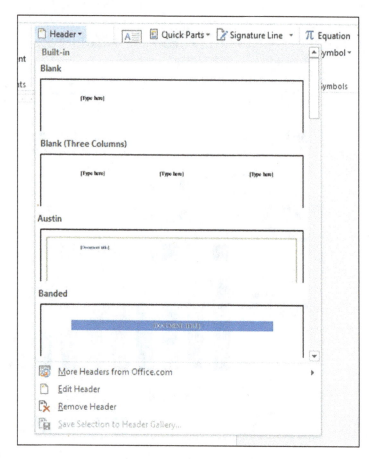

Figure 3.12   Header/ Footer

W3.5.2   Inserting Page Numbering

1. With **Protocol** still selected,

2. Select the **Page Number** drop-down arrow in the **Header/Footer** group of the **Insert** tab, as shown in Figure 3.13.

3. Select **bottom of page** and choose **Plain Number 3**, for page numbering.

4. **Save** and continue to the next section.

Figure 3.13   Page Numbering Command

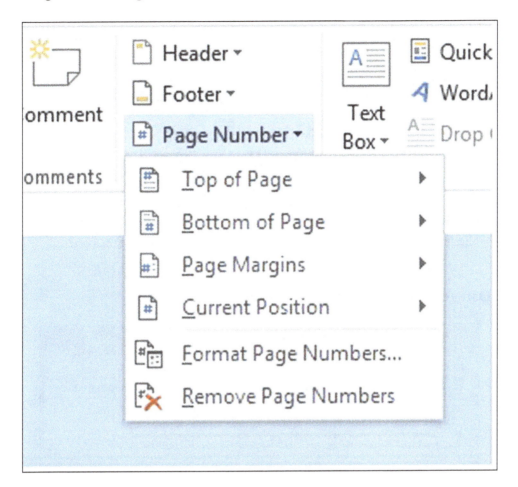

W3.5.3   Inserting Date and Time

1. With **Protocol** still selected.

2. Select the **Date & Time** command from the **Text** group of the **Insert** tab, **as** shown in Figure 3.14.

3. **Choose** your preference from the Date & Time dialog box, as shown in Figure 3.15. (Insert date in the right corner of the **Austin** Header).

4. Click **OK**.

5. **Save** and continue.

Figure 3.14   Date & Time Command

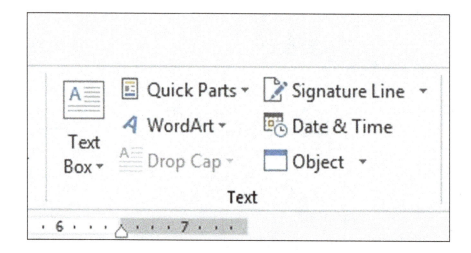

Figure 3.15   Date & Time Dialog Box

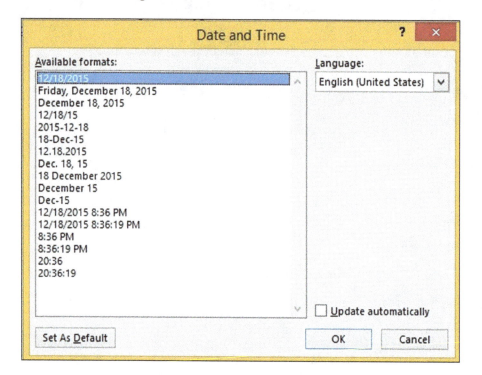

W3.6 Spell Check a Word Document

Word's spell checker proofs a document for spelling and grammatical errors. The grammar checker searches the document for errors in punctuation and word usage. The spell check searches the document for misspelled words and duplicate words.

1. With **Protocol** still selected, proof the document.

2. Select the **Review** tab and select the **Spelling & Grammar** command from the **Proofing** group as shown in Figure 3.16.

3. Click **OK.**

4. **Close** file. (No errors found).

Figure 3.16   Spelling & Grammar Command

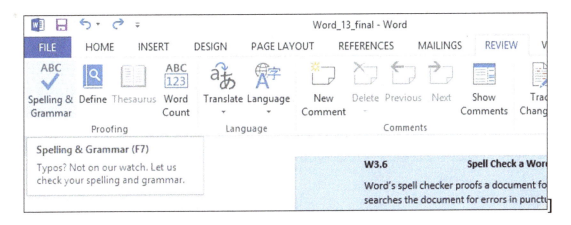

To Correct Spelling Errors

1. Click **Change** to accept the suggestion or **Ignore** to continue reviewing the document and deny the suggested changes, as shown in Figure 3.17.

2. Once Word has completed the **Spelling & Grammatical** check of the document, a dialog box will appear informing you that the Spelling & Grammar check is **complete,** as shown in Figure 3.18.

Figure 3.17   Spelling & Grammar Window Pane

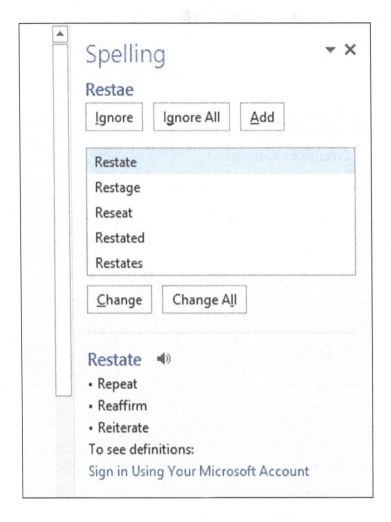

Figure 3.18   Spelling & Grammar Check Complete

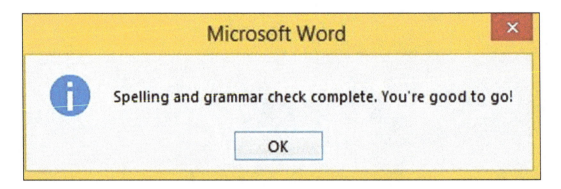

Note: By default, **Word** shows misspelled words with a red wavy line and grammatical errors are shown with a blue wavy line. To correct these errors:

1. Right click the **Spelling** or **Grammatical** error in the document.

2. A menu will appear that offer suggestions for correcting the error; select your desired choice.

3. The correction will appear in the document.

Changing the Spelling Options in Word

1. Select the **File** tab.

2. Click **Options** from the navigation pane on the left.

3. Select **Proofing** to change Word's AutoCorrect options.

4. Click **OK** when finished.

Section 4   Working with Paragraphs in a Word Document

    I.   **Indenting Text**

    II.   **Setting Tabs**

    III. **Inserting Columns**

    IV. **Inserting Page and Section Breaks**

[Student Resource Folder Word_4]

W4.1   Indenting Text in a Document

Word automatically aligns text in a document to the left. One way to change the alignment of text in a document is by indenting the text of a paragraph. Indenting brings structure and sets the paragraph apart in the document. To set a first line indent complete the following.

1. Open the **Marketing** document.

2. Click the **View** tab and make sure the **Ruler** which is located in the **Show** group is checked, as shown in Figure 4.1.

3. To indent the first line, place the insertion point at the beginning of the first paragraph.

4. Slide the **first line indent** marker to the desired position on the ruler (.05 inch). Notice the first line of the paragraph moves in position, as shown in Figure 4.2.

5. Place the insertion point at the beginning of the second paragraph and press tab on the keyboard.

6. **Save** and continue.

Figure 4.1   Ruler

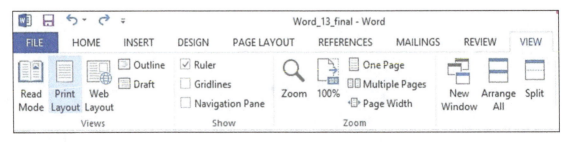

Figure 4.2   First Line Indent

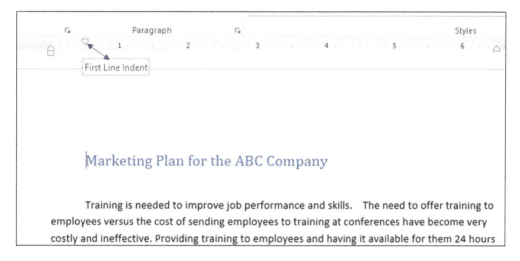

❖ **Note:** Other methods for indenting text can be found in the **Paragraph** group of the **Home** tab and the **Page Layout** tab.

W4.2 Setting Tabs

Tabs provide another option for positioning and aligning text exactly where you want it in the document. The default tabs in Word are set every 0.5 inches. The ruler can be used for manually setting tabs.

1. With the **Marketing** document still open,

2. Show the ruler and make sure the left tab marker (**L**) is displaying on the vertical ruler, as shown in Table 4.1.

3. Select the jobs listed at the bottom of the document. Click to set a (3.5 inch) left tab marker on the horizontal ruler.

4. With the insertion point behind the first word (**Web Developers**), click the tab to move the insertion point to the tab stop at the 3.5 inch marker.

5. Next, click delete from the keyboard to move the word from the next row up, to the insertion point in the document. (**Hint**—You may need to click the delete button twice. This makes two columns for the jobs listed, as shown in Figure 4.3.)

6. Press the down arrow on the keyboard to move to the next line (this places the insertion point behind the next word. (Repeat steps 4–5 until completed).

7. **Save** and **close**.

❖ Customize tab stops can also be set by clicking the drop-down arrow of the **Paragraph Settings** command, in the **Paragraph** group of the **Home** tab.

Table 4.1   Tabs

Left tab ⌊L⌋:	
left aligns text at tab stop	
Center tab ⊥	
center text around tab stop	
Right tab ⌐⌐:	
right aligns text at tab stop	
Decimal tab ⊥:	
aligns decimal numbers at tab stop	
Bar tab ⌐I⌐	
draws a vertical line at tab stop	

Figure 4.3   Two Column Tabs

Web Developers	Project Managers
Software Engineers	Retail Sales
Truck Drivers	Marketing
Physical Therapist	Teachers
Instructional Designers	Registered Nurses

W4.3 Inserting Columns in a Word Document

Columns can change the flow of text and improve the readability of a document. Adding **Columns** to a document will allow text to flow from one column to the next. Columns can be used in brochures or pamphlets. In this example, we will create two columns.

1. Open the **Project Management** document.
2. Select everything on the page before the **Consulting and Development** title, as shown in Figure 4.4
3. Select th**e Page Layout** tab and click the down arrow for the **Columns** command in the **Page Setup** group, as shown in Figure 4.5**.**
4. Select **two** columns. The document will reflect two columns, as shown in Figure 4.6.
5. **Save** work and **continue**.

Figure 4.4   Inserting Columns

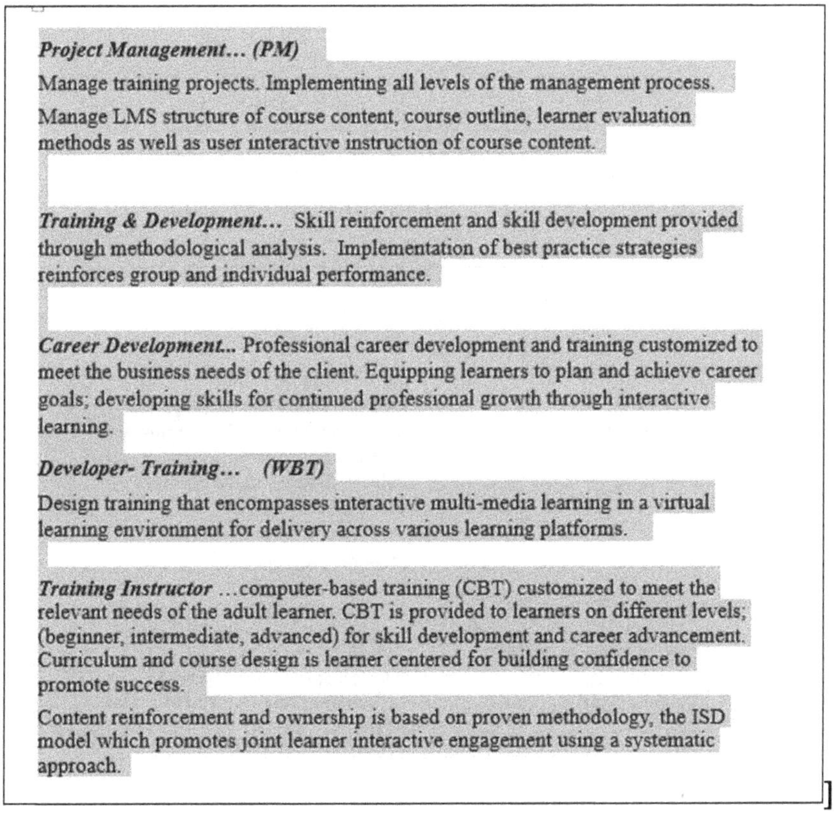

Project Management... (PM)
Manage training projects. Implementing all levels of the management process.
Manage LMS structure of course content, course outline, learner evaluation methods as well as user interactive instruction of course content.

Training & Development... Skill reinforcement and skill development provided through methodological analysis. Implementation of best practice strategies reinforces group and individual performance.

Career Development... Professional career development and training customized to meet the business needs of the client. Equipping learners to plan and achieve career goals; developing skills for continued professional growth through interactive learning.

Developer- Training...   (WBT)
Design training that encompasses interactive multi-media learning in a virtual learning environment for delivery across various learning platforms.

Training Instructor ...computer-based training (CBT) customized to meet the relevant needs of the adult learner. CBT is provided to learners on different levels; (beginner, intermediate, advanced) for skill development and career advancement. Curriculum and course design is learner centered for building confidence to promote success.
Content reinforcement and ownership is based on proven methodology, the ISD model which promotes joint learner interactive engagement using a systematic approach.

Figure 4.5   Setting Columns

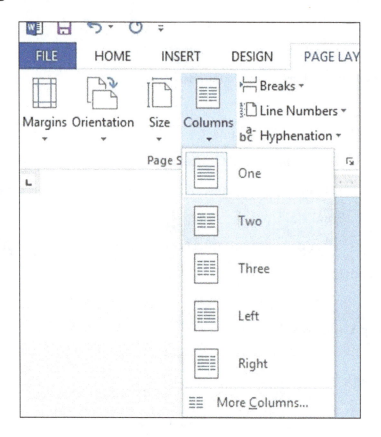

Figure 4.6   Two Columns

Project Management... (PM)

Manage training projects. Implementing all levels of the management process.

Manage LMS structure of course content, course outline, learner evaluation methods as well as user interactive instruction of course content.

Training & Development... Skill reinforcement and skill development provided through methodological analysis. Implementation of best practice strategies reinforces group and individual performance.

Career Development... Professional career development and training customized to meet the business needs of the client. Equipping learners to plan and achieve career goals; developing skills for continued

professional growth through interactive learning.

Developer- Training...   (WBT)

Design training that encompasses interactive multi-media learning in a virtual learning environment for delivery across various learning platforms.

Training Instructor ...computer-based training (CBT) customized to meet the relevant needs of the adult learner. CBT is provided to learners on different levels; (beginner, intermediate, advanced) for skill development and career advancement. Curriculum and course design is learner centered for building confidence to promote success.

Content reinforcement and ownership is based on proven methodology, the ISD model which promotes joint learner interactive engagement using a systematic approach.

W4.4 Inserting Page and Section Breaks

Column Breaks help to determine where each new **Column** begin. **Breaks** in a document are broken down into different sections: **Page Breaks** and **Section Breaks**. The **Page Breaks** section will force text to a new page. However, **Section Breaks** allow each section of a document to have a different format. In this section we will insert a section break and a page break.

1. With **Project Management** still open,

2. Place the insertion point in front of the title **Developer Training** in column two.

3. Select the **Page Layout** tab. Click the **Breaks** command, located in the **Page Setup** group.

4. Choose **Column** from the drop-down menu, shown in Figure 4.7.

   ❖ Notice, the title moved to the top of the column, as shown in Figure 4.8.

5. Next, place the insertion point in front of the title, **Consulting and Development.**

6. Select **page** from the **Page Breaks** category to apply a page break, as shown in Figure 4.9.

Notice the selected text now moves to the next page as shown in Figure 4.10

7. **Save** and **close** document.

   ❖ To show all breaks in the document, click the **Home** tab, select the **Show/Hide** command in the **Paragraph** group.

Figure 4.7   Inserting Column Breaks

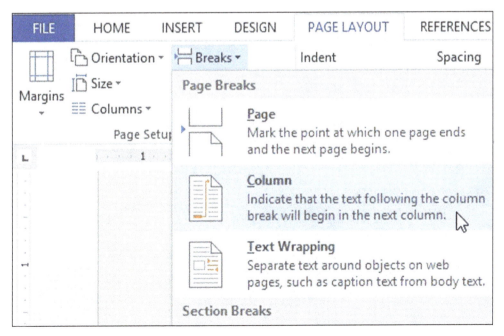

Figure 4.8   Column Breaks

Project Management... (PM)
Manage training projects.
Implementing all levels of the
management process.
Manage LMS structure of course
content, course outline, learner
evaluation methods as well as user
interactive instruction of course
content.

Training & Development... Skill
reinforcement and skill development
provided through methodological
analysis. Implementation of best
practice strategies reinforces group
and individual performance.

Career Development... Professional
career development and training
customized to meet the business needs
of the client. Equipping learners to
plan and achieve career goals;
developing skills for continued
professional growth through
interactive learning.

Developer- Training...   (WBT)
Design training that encompasses
interactive multi-media learning in a
virtual learning environment for
delivery across various learning
platforms.

Training Instructor ...computer-
based training (CBT) customized to
meet the relevant needs of the adult
learner. CBT is provided to learners
on different levels; (beginner,
intermediate, advanced) for skill
development and career advancement.
Curriculum and course design is
learner centered for building
confidence to promote success.
Content reinforcement and ownership
is based on proven methodology, the
ISD model which promotes joint
learner interactive engagement using
a systematic approach.

Consulting and Development

Figure 4.9   Page Breaks

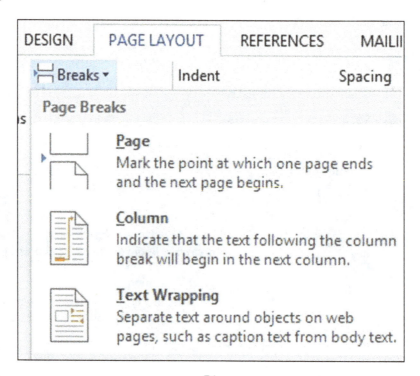

Figure 4.10   Column Break (Showing·Formatting)

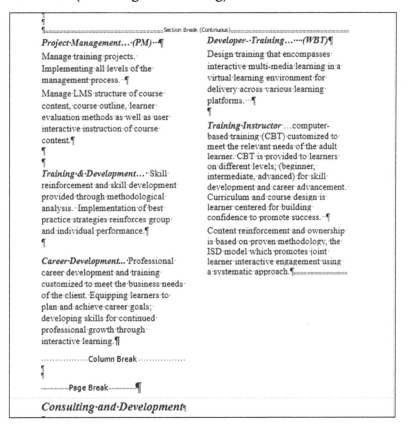

Section 5   Working with Objects in a Word Document

    I.   **Inserting WordArt**

   II.   **Inserting Pictures**

  III.   **Inserting Text Boxes**

  IV.   **Inserting SmartArt**

   V.   **Inserting Tables**

  VI.   **Inserting Charts**

[Student Resource Folder Word_5]

W5.1 Inserting WordArt

WordArt is a great way to add special effects and style to your text while making it stand out in your document. **WordArt** works well for many things including creating logos, stationary, or flyers.

1. Open a **blank** document.

2. Click the **Insert** tab, and select the **WordArt** command, located in the **Text** group.

3. Choose a desired **WordArt** style and type *Coldest Places to Live*, and center WordArt at the top of the document as shown in Figure 5.1.

    ❖ Use the **Drawing Tools Format** tab to customize and format WordArt to your satisfaction. You can change the text styles, effect, font, and alignment. Select from the many different options available for fill patterns and customization that includes shadow and three-dimensional effects with many others to choose from.

4. **Save** document as **Weather** and continue.

Figure 5.1   **WordArt**

Coldest Places to Live

W5.2 Inserting Pictures

Pictures added to a document help give meaning and bring words to life. **Pictures** can be added to your document from your computer, online, or from a file. In this exercise we will insert a **Picture** from a computer file.

1. With the **Weather** document open,
2. Click the **Insert** tab.
3. Place the insertion point slightly under the title where you would like the image to appear.
4. Click the **Insert** tab and select **Pictures** from the **Illustrations** group, as shown in Figure 5.2.
5. The **Insert Pictures** dialog box opens, as shown in Figure 5.3.
6. Insert the image from your Word resource 5 folder into the document. To modify the image select the **Picture Tools Format** tab. Choose from a list of formatting options such as resizing and cropping. Change the style of the image and view other image formatting options that are available.
7. **Save** work and continue.

Figure 5.2   Inserting Pictures

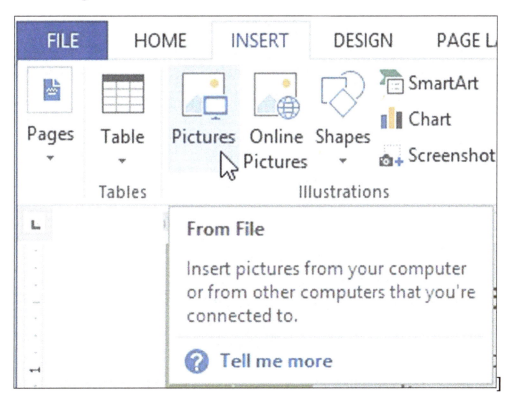

Figure 5.3   Insert Picture Dialog Box

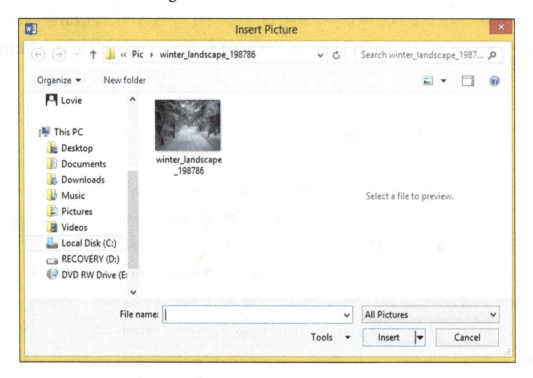

W5.2.1   Wrapping Text around an Image

Once a **Picture** is inserted into a document the image is by default set to **In Line with Text**. Therefore, changing the **text wrapping style** for an image will allow you to do two things with the image. First, changing the **text wrapping style** of an image will allow you to freely move the image to a different location in the document. Also, changing the **text wrapping style** of an image will give you more flexibility with wrapping the text around the image.

1. Select the inserted image, notice the **Picture Tools Format** tab appears.
2. Click the down arrow for the **Wrap Tex**t command in the **Arrange** group.
3. Scroll with the mouse over the different **text wrapping** style options. (Note: a **live preview** of the different **text wrapping** styles will appear in the document).
4. Choose your desired **text wrapping** style. (**Note:** you may also right click the image to move it and select the **wrap text** command). Choose **tight.**

> **Hint**: the **Position** command of the **Arrange** group will also allow you to choose where the selected image will appear in the document, and it will automatically wrap the text for you in the document.

W5.3 Inserting Text Boxes

Text boxes can be placed anywhere in your document. They can be colorful to add emphasis to your text or have different shapes and style effects. Word has several predesigned text box options to choose from or you may create your own.

1. With the **Weather** document still open,
2. Click the **Insert** tab.
3. Select the **Text Box** command, from the **Text** group, as shown in Figure 5.4.
4. Choose the **draw text box** option. (Draw the text box and center it near the bottom of the image, as shown in Figure 5.5).
5. Click inside the text box to **type the name of your image**. (Click outside of the text box to deselect it).
6. **Save** work and continue.

Note: Expand the size of the text box to view text inside. Text box must be selected to modify the shape, style, and size.

Figure 5.4   Text Box

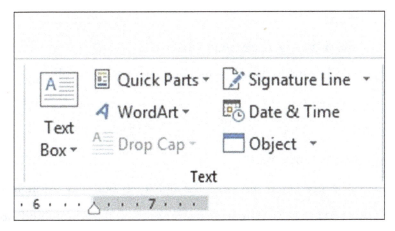

Figure 5.5   Inserted Text Box

W5.3.1   Delete a text box

1. Click the border of the text box that you want to delete and press **delete**.

W5.3.2   Remove the border from a text box.

1. Select the border of the text box.

2. Click on the **format** tab of the **drawing tools** contextual tab.

3. Select the down arrow of the **Shape Outline** command in the **Shape Styles** group and click **No Outline,** as shown in.

W5.4   Inserting SmartArt in a Word Document

Information in a document can be presented not only through text, but also through a visual representation of graphics, such as **SmartArt**. SmartArt offers many ways of illustrating and presenting data. Organizational charts can be used to present data in a hierarchical structure format with different diagrams and categories to choose from.

1. With the **weather** document selected,

2. Click the **Insert** tab and click the **SmartArt** button located in the **Illustrations** group.

Step 2 SmartArt Command

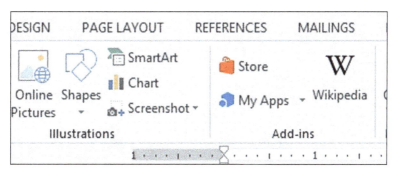

3. From the **Choose a SmartArt Graphic** dialog box, select the **Relationship** tab, and choose the **Plus and Minus** SmartArt.

4. Click **OK**.

5. The **SmartArt** will appear in the document.

6. Position the insertion point inside the [*Text*] placeholder of the SmartArt and type *Adjustable, Challenging*. Use the **SmartArt Format Tools** tab to make changes or modifications to the **shape style** or **layout** of the object.

7. Center the SmartArt in the center of the document under the image, as shown in Figure 5.6.

8. **Save** work and continue.

Hint: Moving the **SmartArt** requires that you position the pointer on the diagram border until the pointer displays with a four-headed arrow. Left click with the mouse, hold and drag the diagram to the desired new location.

Note: **Height** and **Width** can be changed by expanding the borders of the diagram. To maintain the diagrams proportions, hold down the **Shift key** while dragging the borders of the diagram to increase or decrease to the desired size.

Figure 5.6   SmartArt Inserted

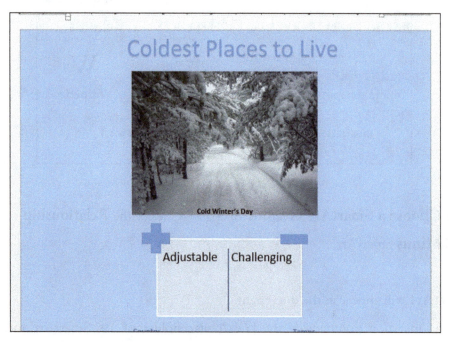

W5.5 Inserting Tables

Tables can be inserted in Word to display data in a column and row format. When creating tables in Word there are several different options to choose from for your design and layout.

Tables can be used to hold **text** or **numerical** data. There is also an option to convert text to a table.

1. With the **Weather** document still open.

2. Place the insertion point under the SmartArt graphic to insert the table.

3. Click the **Insert** tab and select **Table** from the **Tables** group. (A drop-down menu will appear).

4. Move your mouse, (**hover**) over the **cell** grids and a **Live Preview** will appear displaying a **Table** view in your document.

5. Choose a **2x6** table. Left click **once** or press **enter** from the keyboard to have the **Table** inserted into the document.

6. Center the table so that it aligns with the other objects on the page.

7. Click inside the cell of the table to enter data. Type the information from Table 5.1 below into the table**.**

8. Press the tab key to advance to the next **cell** in the **Table.**

9. Click the **Design** and **Format** tab of the **Table Tools** contextual tab to modify or make changes to the table.

10. Click away from the **table** to deselect it.

11. **Save** and close.

❖ Position all objects to fit on 1 page.

Table 5.1   **Table Data**

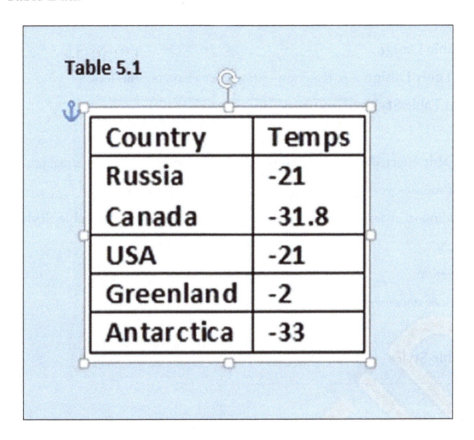

W5.5.1   Modifying Tables in a Word Document

Once a table has been added to your document, you may need to make some modification to it such as: **Add a row or column** to the table or **Delete a row or column** from your table.

1. To **add a row or column**, right click in the column or row of the table. (A submenu will appear).

2. Notice the arrow next to the **Insert** command, displaying other optional views for inserting rows or columns into the table.

3. Select the desired option, and the new row or column will appear.

To delete a row or column from your table:

1. Select the row or column in the table, right click and click **Delete Cells.**
2. Notice the **Delete Cells** dialog box pops up.
3. Click to **Delete entire row** or **Delete entire column.**
4. Click **OK**, when finished. (The **column** or **row** will be deleted).

Changing the Table Design:

In the **Table Tools Design** tab, there are options for changing the look of your table. Choose from Word's predesigned **Table Styles** or customize your own.

1. With the **Table** selected, click the **Design** tab of the **Table Tools** contextual tab.
2. Hover your mouse over the different **Table Styles** for a **Live Preview**.
3. To view additional styles, click the **more** down-pointing arrow in the **Table Styles** group, as shown in Figure 5.8.
4. Make a selection.
5. **Save** and close document.

Figure 5.8   Table Styles

Changing the Table Layout:

❖ Word's **Table Tools Layout** tab offers additional options for customizing the **Table's Layout**. Some changes include changing the cell size, changing the alignment and changing the margins. To make changes to the Layout of the Table, click the **Layout** tab appearing on the **Table Tools** contextual tab.

W5.6   Inserting Charts in a Word Document

Data can be presented in a visual format and displayed graphically. **Charts** can provide a visual meaning and understanding of the data in your document. Word has several types of charts to choose from that will effectively transcend your expectations.

Word uses a spreadsheet, similar to that of Excel, as a placeholder for entering the numerical data into your document. (Learn more about charts in the **Excel** section).

1. Reopen the **Weather** document.
2. Place the insertion point under the table on the page.
3. Click the **Insert** tab and select the **Chart** command in the **Illustrations** group. (An **Insert Chart** dialog box appears).
4. Select the **column** chart tab and choose the **stacked column** type.
5. Click **OK**.
6. A chart and placeholder spreadsheet appears in the document, as shown in Figure 5.9.
7. Enter your data into the spreadsheet's placeholder from the table in the document. (This is your data source of information), as shown in Figure 5.10.
8. Click **X** to close the spreadsheet when finished.
9. Position all objects to fit on 1 page, as shown in Figure 5.11.
10. **Save** and **close**.

Note: Right click the **Chart** and select **edit data** for the placeholder's spreadsheet to reappear or to change the **Chart's Format and Design.**

Figure 5.9   Chart Placeholder

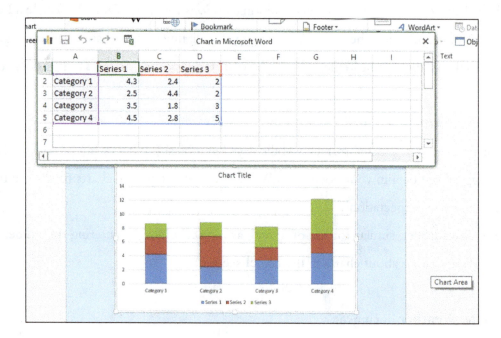

Figure 5.10   Chart Data

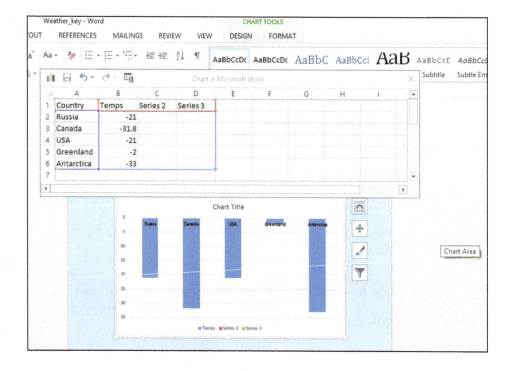

Figure 5.11   Completed Document

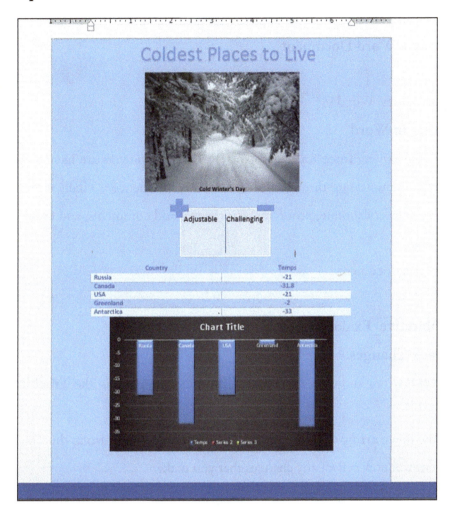

Section 6   Working with Advanced Features in Word

I.   **Collaborating in Word**

II.   **Protecting a Word Document**

W6.1 Collaborating in Word

As technology is the driving force for today's society, many employers are having their employees work remotely. Effectively communicating through document correspondence is vitally important. Word features a tool that will allow you to collaborate, proof, make revisions, add comments, and **track changes** made to a document electronically.

To track changes in a document:

1.   Open the **Objective_Ex** document.

2.   Turn on **Track Changes.**

3.   Select the **Review** tab and click the **Track Changes** command in the **Tracking** group, as seen in Figure 6.1.

4.   Next, click the down arrow to select the **All Markup** command, also in the Tracking group.

5.   The document will now reflect any changes that you make.

   ❖   Note the comments from another reviewer.

Figure 6.1   Track Changes Command

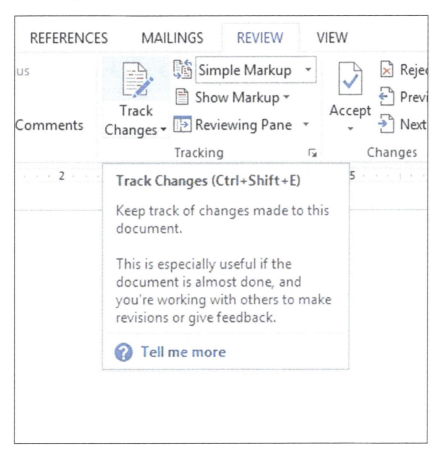

W6.1.1   Viewing Track Changes

Any changes made to the document will appear as a colored **markup** in the document. Once text is marked for deletion, it will appear crossed out in the document or underlined so all changes are tracked by each reviewer. (**Note:** this is dependent upon which **balloons** are selected in the **Show Markup** command). **Text** added to the document will appear **underlined**.

1. Select the word **Discuss**, and press **delete** from the keyboard.
2. Type *Create*. View changes, shown in Figure 6.2.
3. **Continue.**

Figure 6.2   Show Markup

> **Course Objectives:**
>
> 1. ~~Discuss~~ Create in at least five sentences, their expectations for successful projects and develop
> means of implementing them through improved planning, communication, and project monitoring, as
> described in the workshop.
>
> 2. Describe a minimum of five tools and methods that can be used to better understand the client
> they serve, using the job requirements described in the project charter.

W6.1.2   Adding Comments

To add comments to the document

1. Select the text, **ISD** in item 3 of the document.
2. Click the **New Comment** command in the **Comments** group of the **Review** tab, as shown in Figure 6.3.
3. Type *no abbreviations* in the comment section. (Click outside the comment box when finished).
4. **Comment** will appear in the document.
5. **Continue.**

Figure 6.3   New Comment

W6.1.3   Deleting Comments

To delete comments from the document

1. Select the comment, [**ISD**].
2. Right click on the **comment** and click **delete comment** from the sub-menu.

3. Comment will be deleted.

4. **Save** and continue.

W6.1.4 Accepting/Rejecting Track Changes

In order to make any of the comments or suggestions offered in the document become permanent, you must **Accept** or **Reject** the suggested changes.

1. Select the comment, **create**, in the document.

2. Select the **Accept** command, shown in Figure 6.4.

3. Notice the *markup disappears* from the document. The suggested change was made to the document and Word advances to the next tracked change in the document.

4. Continue advancing through the document until all **markups** have been either **Accepted** or **Rejected**.

5. When you have finished checking the document, turn off **Track Changes.**

6. **Save** work and **exit.**

Figure 6.4   Accept/Reject Changes

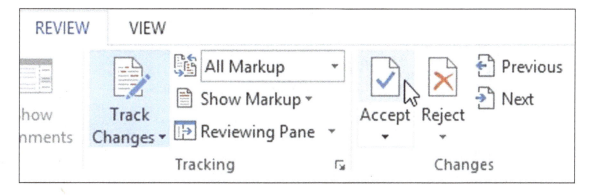

W6.2 Protecting a Word Document

Word offers protection for working on documents that may be confidential and to ensure only authorized users have access to your documents.

1. Click the **File** tab.

2. From the **Info** navigation pane, select **Protect Document**, a drop-down menu appears. Select **Encrypt with Password,** as shown in Figure 6.5.

3. Notice an **Encrypt Document** dialog box opens, prompting for a password. (Enter a password.)

4. A confirmation of password dialog box reopens for you to reenter the password.

5. After the password confirmation is completed, Word informs you the document is now password protected.

Figure 6.5   Protect Document

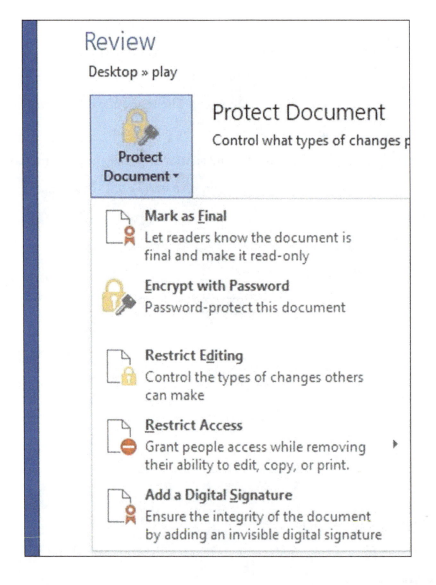

Index

Word 2013

Knowledge and Skill Assessment

W1   Knowledge Check

1. Word has several ways to view a document, but _____ _____ shows how the document would look before printing.

2. The _____ tab gives access to backstage.

3. Click the _____button on the ribbon to exit Word without going backstage.

4. To view commands that are not visible on the **Quick Access Toolbar**, select the _____ commands.

5. Print Preview and Print is a command that can be added to the Quick Access Toolbar? True or False _____.

6. The ____ _____ _____ can show above or below the ribbon.

7. To customize the Ribbon, click the _____ command backstage.

W2   Knowledge Check

1. Templates are _____ documents.

2. The page orientation has two layout types, Portrait and _____.

3. Custom margins can be located in the _____ group of the Page Layout tab.

4. _____ is Word's default margin settings.

5. The default paper size in Word is set to _____ size.

6. Templates have _____ that hold a place for text to be entered.

7. Click the _____ button, which **opens** the dialog box to locate existing documents.

W3   Knowledge Check

1. Selected text will be _____ in a document.

2. Text that is selected can be deleted. (True/False)

3. Copied text is placed on the _____ for later use.

4. After text is cut from the document, _____ inserts the text into another location of the document.

5. **Page Number** appears in the _____ _____group.

6. The **cut** command is located in the ____group.

7. **Font Color** is located in the _____ group.

W4   Knowledge Check

1. The **First Line Indent** marker can be positioned on the ____ to indent the first line of paragraphs in the document.

2. **Section Breaks** can be inserted by clicking the _____ command.

3. Customize tab stops can be set with the ____ _____ command.

4. Click the _____ command to insert columns into the document.

5. The _____ _____ left aligns text at the tab stop.

6. Tabs can be set manually on the _____.

7. Click ____ ____ tab to view the **page break** options.

W5   Knowledge Check

1. Click the ____ tab to access the WordArt command.

2. Click the ____ command to insert pictures from a file.

3. The ___ _____ command allows you to draw your own text box in the document.

4. The **wrap text** command is located in the arrange group of the format tab on the _____ _____ contextual tab.

5. The **SmartArt** command is located in the _____ group.

6. The ____ ____ shows a view of the table before it is inserted into the document.

7. The _____ command allows you to insert charts into the document.

Skill Assessments 1 and 2

(Modify a Word Template)
[Student Resource File—(SkillAssessment_2)]

1. Open the **Certificate of Participation** template.

2. Select the placeholder [**Recipient Name**] and enter **Your Name**.

3. Select the placeholder [**Team Name**] and replace it with **Word-2013**.

4. Select the placeholder [**Signature Name**], replace it with **Management.**

5. Select the placeholder [**Click to select a date**], pull the arrow down and select the **current date**.

6. **Save** as **MyCertificate**.

7. **Preview** then **print** document in Landscape.

8. **Close** document.

Skill Assessment 3

(Create a Memo, Insert a Table, Insert Page Header/Footer)

1. Create a simple memo with 2–3 sentences.

2. Include a heading for the memo that includes the following: **To, From, Date, Re**.

3. Create a table and insert it in the memo, with the schedule changes from Table 3 below.

4. Include a **header/footer** with the **[Date, Page Number],** and you determine where it should be placed in the document.

5. **Spell check** the document.

6. **Preview** and **print** the document.

7. **Save** as **Memo.docx**.

8. **Close** document.

Table 3

Course#	Course	Delivery	Time	Days
DR-101	Drama	Classroom	6pm-9pm	MW
PSY-101	Psychology	Blended	12-2pm	Tue/Thur
HIS-101	History	Blended	9am-10am	MWF
ENG-101	English	Online	N/A	N/A

Skill Assessment 4

(Create a Two-Column Newsletter, Insert and Modify a Shape Object)

[Student Resource File—(SkillAssessment_4)]

1. Open the **Wellness** document.

2. Create a one-page newsletter with two columns. Column two should begin with **Who is at risk**?.

3. Insert an **image** and place it next to the topic, **How to pick sunscreen**. You determine the image.

4. Insert a new subheading titled, **Safety Tips**, at the bottom of the newsletter in column two.

5. Insert a **wave shape** and place it under the new subheading. Add text to the wave shape that reads, **For best results, apply sunscreen 30 minutes before exposure to sun**.

6. **Preview** document to make sure it all fits on one page, (in portrait) and **print.**

7. **Save** and **close** document.

Skill Assessment 5

(Modify a Business Letter, Include First Line Indent, Insert Page Break, and Insert Table and WordArt)

[Student Resource File—(SkillAssessment_5)

1. Open the **HAT** document.

2. Select the title of the document, **HAT**, and delete.

3. Create a new title for the document with **WordArt.** (Keeping the same title name).

4. Insert a **First Line Indent** for each paragraph at the .05 inch marker.

5. Insert a **page break** at the beginning of the text titled, [**HAT's Mission . . .**].

6. Copy the text, **Provide**, from the Mission's phrase.

7. Paste it in front of the **3rd** mission statement before the word **Workers**] to make the 3rd mission bullet read: **Provide Workers Soft Skill Training Improvement**.

8. Put a **1-inch tab** setting for the 3 mission statements. (**Hint**: show the ruler and select the three phrases before setting the tab on the ruler).

9. Add your choice of **bullets** to the three mission statements.

10. Create a **table** that displays the *Center's Hours of Operation* from Table 5 below. Place the table under the HAT's Mission on page two of the document.

11. Format all headers in the table with **bold** text.

12. **Save** and **close** the document.

Table 5

Column Headers – [Days of Week], [Hours of Operation], [Training Hours], [Lab Hours]

Hours of Operation - M-F (8am – 5: pm) - Saturday – 9am – 1pm- Closed - Sunday

Training Hours – Monday-Thursday – (9am-3pm) -   Friday – (9am-1pm)

Lab Hours – Monday-Thursday – (9am – 3pm)   - Friday – (9am - 1pm) – Saturday – (9-12 noon)

<h1 style="text-align:center">Word Answer Key</h1>

Answer W1

1. Print Preview
2. File
3. Close (X)
4. More
5. True
6. Quick Access Toolbar
7. Options

Answer W2

1. Predesigned
2. Landscape
3. Page Setup
4. Normal
5. Letter
6. Placeholders
7. Browse

Answer W3

1. Highlighted
2. True
3. Clipboard
4. Paste
5. Header & Footer
6. Clipboard
7. Font

Answer W4

1. Ruler
2. Breaks
3. Paragraph Settings
4. Columns
5. Left tab
6. Ruler
7. Page Layout

Answer W5

1. Insert
2. Pictures
3. Text Box
4. Picture Tools
5. Illustrations
6. Live Preview
7. Chart

Excel 2013

Excel is a spreadsheet application that stores information in text or numerical format, and it can be used to perform mathematical calculations. Data in the worksheet are entered into columns and rows. Once information is stored into a worksheet; it is then saved in what is called a workbook. Many organizations use Excel to organize and analyze data.

This tutorial will help you to improve your skills, knowledge and abilities with the Excel application. Lessons are designed to guide you through the essentials and then introduce you to some advanced concepts that are relevant to the workforce.

Excel 2013

Section I   Excel Essentials

E1.1   Open a Blank Excel Workbook

1. To open Excel, tap or click the start screen button in the lower left corner of the screen.

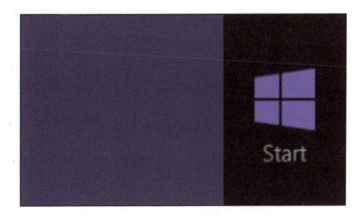

2. From the start screen, begin typing the word **Excel.** (The search panel will open).

3. Select the **Blank workbook.**

4. A **new** workbook will open.

Step 3   Blank Workbook

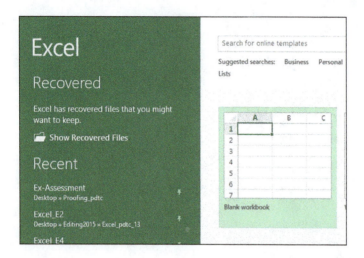

E1.2   Excel Graphical User Interface (GUI)

In order to interact with the common tasks in Excel you would need to become familiar with the interface shown below in Figure 1.1. View the **Excel** screen and identify the basic features.

Compare and contrast the screen in Figure 1.1 with your screen.

Refer to Table 1.1 for a description of Excel features.

Figure 1.1   Excel GUI

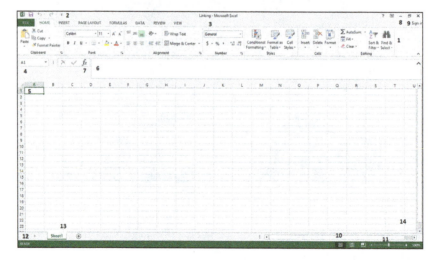

Table 1.1   GUI Excel Features and Descriptions

Indicator	Features	Description
1	Ribbon	Tabs are on top. Groups are on bottom and commands are in between.
2	Quick Access Toolbar	Common tasks button
3	Title Bar	Shows name of document and application name.
4	Name Box	Displays active cell address
5	Active Cell	Indicates the active cell in the worksheet that will display typed data
6	Formula Bar	Displays the formula or cell data stored in the active cell.
7	Insert Function	Starts the function and opens function dialog box.
8	Minimize button	Minimize the screen
9	Restore button	Restores the screen
10	Workbook views	Ways of viewing document (Read Mode, Print Layout View, Web Layout View).
11	Zoom Indicator	Document viewing adjustment.
12	Status bar	Displays document information (pages, word count. Right click the status bar to customize it.
13	Worksheets or Spreadsheets	Hold the content of the data for the workbook.
14	Horizontal/Vertical scroll	Displays screen content beyond what fits on the screen view.

E1.3   Exploring the Ribbon

The **Ribbon** is designed with **Tab** buttons on top and **Group** associated commands on the bottom. These commands allow you access to **Excel's** common tasks. The **Ribbon** can be customized to add your daily personal **tabs** and **group** commands.

The **file** tab located on the ribbon is sometimes referred to as **backstage view.** This was a term that was used when Microsoft replaced the Office Button in the 2007 version. Printing, saving, and exporting are just a few of the many options available from this tab selection.

Note: Contextual Tabs are also displayed on the ribbon. However, **contextual tabs** only appear when an object is selected to give further command options for working with that particular object.

To customize the tabs on the Ribbon:

1. Click the **file** tab to access backstage viewing.
2. Click **Options** from the navigation pane on the left, as shown in Figure 1.2
3. Select **Customize Ribbon** from the navigation on the left. On the right, (under the heading, **customize the ribbon**), select **new tab** (at the bottom of the dialog box).

4. Select the **new tab** and click **rename**. Enter a name for the new tab in the dialog box that appears, as shown in Figure 1.3.

❖ **Note:** the new tab and new group appears together, as a set.

5. Next, select **new group** and click the rename tab to give the new group a name of your choice, (a **rename** dialog box will open with an *option* to choose an image).

6. With your new group selected, choose your group associated commands, (these are the commands that you use regularly such as the font, font size, the format painter, paste . . .).

7. Select your commands from the choices on the left and **add** them to your new group on the right.

8. Click **OK** when finished.

Step 1   File Tab

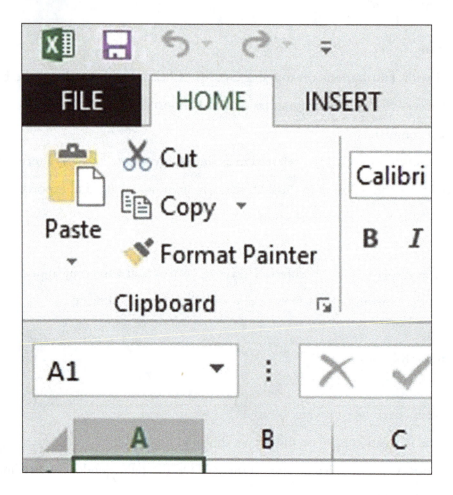

Figure 1.2   Options

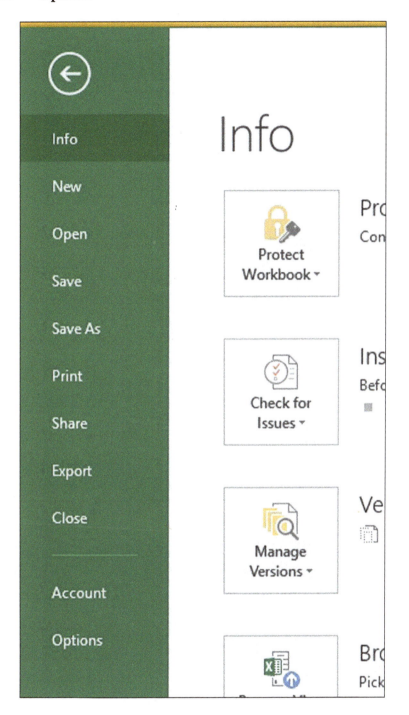

Figure 1.3   Customizing the Ribbon

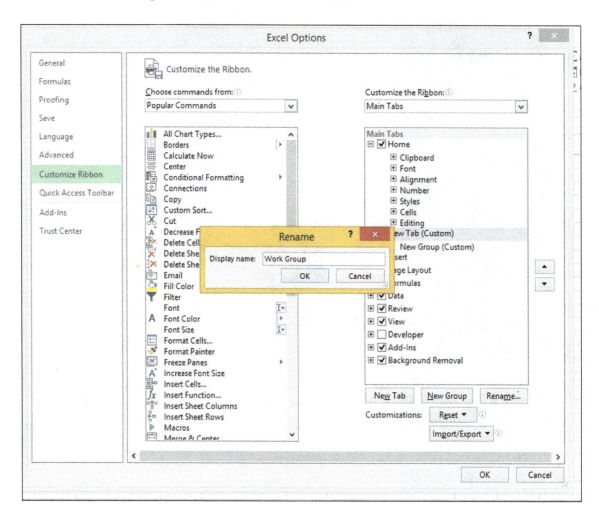

1. To **Show/Hide** the Ribbon, click the up pointing arrow above the ribbon and make a selection. See Figure 1.4

Figure 1.4   Show/Hide Ribbon

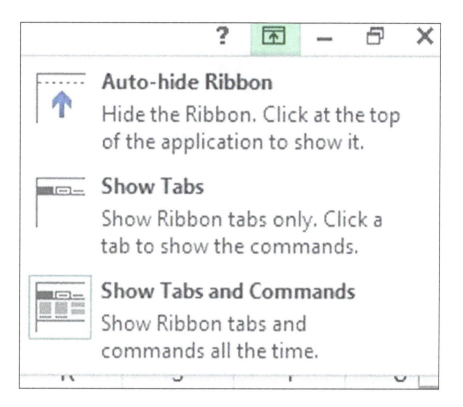

E1.4   Customizing the Quick Access Toolbar

The **Quick Access Toolbar** allows you to add commands that are accessed on a daily basis much quicker.

1. In order to access the **Quick Access Toolbar**, click the drop-down arrow to the right of the **Access Toolbar**, either (**above or below the ribbon**), depending on the location of your quick access toolbar. See Figure 1.5.

2. Select the commands that you wish to have added to your **Quick Access Toolbar.**

❖ In order to choose more commands; click the **More Commands** option and select the commands to **add** to your Quick Access Toolbar.

Figure 1.5   Quick Access Toolbar

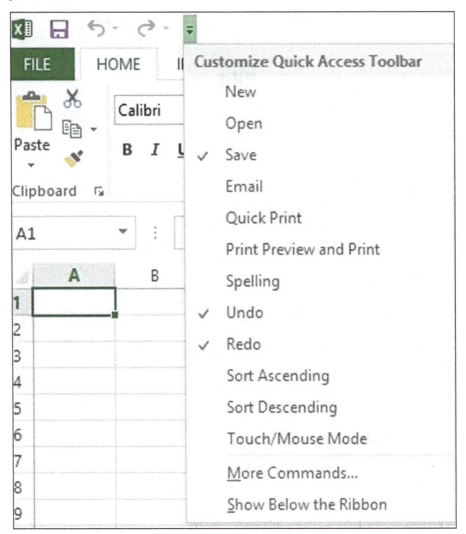

E1.5   Excel Help Feature

The **Help** feature displays information on Excel. Click the question mark **[?]** located in the top right corner of the screen. Enter a word or phrase to search and a list of topics will be displayed. You can also access the help option by pressing **F1** from your keyboard.

Section 2   Creating an Excel Workbook

I.   Opening a New Excel Workbook

II.   Opening an Existing Workbook

III.   Working with Excel Templates

IV.   Entering Content in an Excel Worksheet

V.   Entering Formulas in Excel

VI.   Copying and Pasting Formulas

VII.   Saving an Excel Workbook

VIII.   Page Layout and Excel Printing Options (PDF)

IX.   Closing/Exiting Excel

[Student Resource Folder—(Excel_resource_E2)

E2.1   Open a New Excel Workbook

1. From the desktop, click the **File** tab.

2. Select **New**, click **Blank Workbook**.

3. A **new blank workbook** opens.

E2.2   Open an Existing Workbook

In order to retrieve documents that were previously saved on your computer or external drive:

1. Click the **File** tab**.**

2. Select **Open** from the navigation pane on the left, as shown in Figure 2.1.

3. Click **Computer** then **browse** to locate the existing file.

4. **Select** the existing file from the **Open** dialog box, as shown in Figure 2.2. (**Note**: to open workbooks that were previously opened, browse the **recent workbooks** instead of browsing through your computer files).

5. Click **Open.**

Figure 2.1   Opening Existing Document

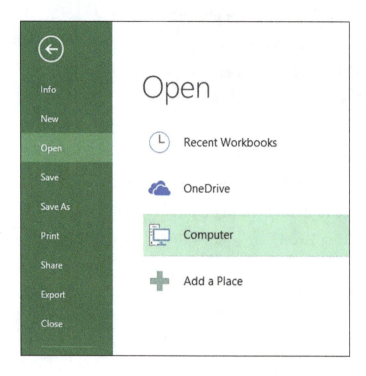

Figure 2.2   Open Dialog Box

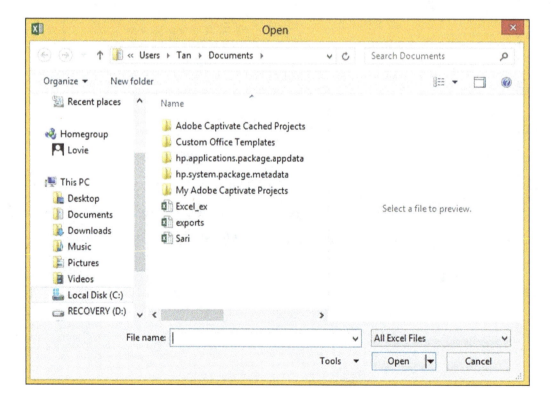

E2.3 Working with Excel Templates

Predesigned workbooks are called **templates. Templates** have customized designs and formatting to save you time. To access **Excel** templates:

1. Click the **File** tab.
2. Click **New**; notice a display of **Templates** appears.
3. Select a **Template** to preview then click **Create** to download the desired template. See Figure 2.3.
4. Workbook opens with the selected **Template**.

Step 2   New Tab

Figure 2.3   Excel Templates

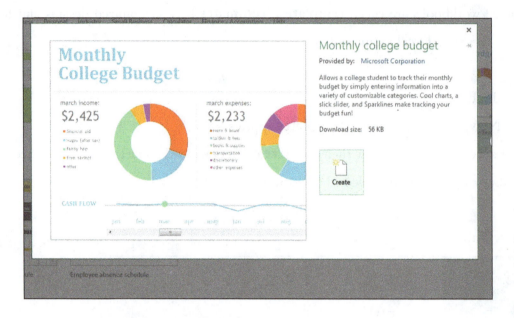

E2.4   Entering Content in an Excel Worksheet

Excel allows text and numbers to be entered into the **cells** of a spreadsheet. All cells have a cell address. **Cell Addresses** are identified first by the **column** and second by the **row**. **Columns** are vertical and are identified by the letters of the alphabets (A, B, C . . .). **Rows** are horizontal and are referenced and identified by numbers (1, 2, 3 . . .). See Figure 2.4.

1. Open a **blank workbook**.
2. Notice the **active cell**, (the cell with the rectangle box around it) by default is **A1**.
3. Click in the cell to select it and type your name. (**Note**: content shows in the cell and in the **Formula Bar,** as shown in Figure 2.5.

Hint: A cell must be active, (selected) to enter content. . . Column headers and row headers are selected when a cell becomes active, and the **cell address** will appear in the **Name Box**.

❖ **Note**: This tutorial uses the *A1 reference style*.

Figure 2.4   Cell Address

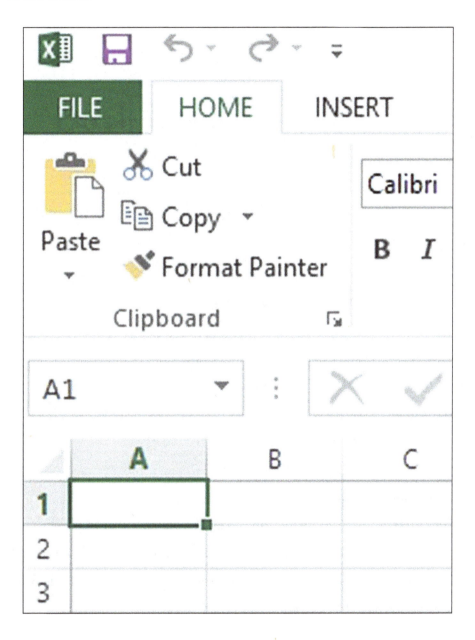

Figure 2.5   Range

Selecting a Range of Cells

1. Left click in cell **A1**, hold and drag across cells **A1:C7**;

2. Release mouse when range of cells are highlighted, as shown in Figure 2.5.

Deleting Cell Content

1. Select cell **A1** (where your name was typed).

2. Press **delete** from the keyboard.

3. Contents in cell will be deleted.

E2.5   Entering Formulas in Excel

Excel applies **formulas** to perform mathematical calculations in a worksheet. **Formulas** in Excel are entered into a cell and always begin with an equal $(=)$ sign. Add the cell address (for each value), separated by the mathematical operator needed to perform the calculation. In our example, we will use the mathematical operator addition, $(+)$ to perform the calculation and find Pham's Total Surcharge.

1. Open the **Excel_E2** workbook.

2. Select the **Sum Function** worksheet.

3. Click in cell **I3**.

4. Type $=E3+F3+G3+H3$.

5. Press the **Enter** key.

❖ **The result, ($7370.00) is displayed in cell I3.** (arrow up or click in cell **I3** to view results)

❖ **Notice that each cell referenced in the formula is highlighted for proof.**

Hint: To view or modify the formula reselect cell **I3**. Make changes to the formula in the **Formula Bar**.

E2.6 Copying and Pasting Formulas

The **clipboard** is where items are placed when they are copied. Items placed on the clipboard can be pasted as many times as necessary, and they can also be pasted in any open document. Clipboard items are available until you choose to discard them or exit the workbook.

When **copying** from one cell location to another cell location, the data is automatically copied to the Clipboard. Once the formula is pasted, Excel will update the column/row letters or numbers to reflect the change in the new cell address and location. This is known as **relative addressing** (the cell address changes with respect to the destination address).

(**Note**: the cell where the formula originates is known as the source, and the cell where the formula is pasted is called the destination.)

1. With the **Sum Function** worksheet still selected,
2. Click in cell **I3.**
3. Click the **Copy** command in the **Clipboard** group of the **Home** tab, as shown in Figure 2.8. (Notice a rotating rectangle encloses the cell to be copied).
4. Select cell **I4** to paste the contents, as shown in Figure 2.6.
5. Click the **Paste** command in the **Clipboard** group of the **Home** tab. (Notice the contents are pasted in the selected cell and the relative address changed.

❖ **Note:** in this example, the relative address (cell reference) changed with respect to the row; the columns remained the same.

6. **Save** and continue.

Figure 2.6   Copy Formula

	Dynasty Resort								
	Guest F Name	Guest Last Name	# Days	Room Rate	Room Charge	Amenities	Surcharges	Valet	Total Bill Due
3	Kim	Pham	7	$700.00	$4,900.00	$470.00	$1,250.00	$750.00	$7,370.00
4	George	Gorman	7	$1,200.00	$8,400.00	$650.00	$1,750.00	$250.00	
5	Mike	Davis	6	$1,500.00	$9,000.00	$950.00	$1,950.00	$950.00	
6	Jan	Nelson	7	$1,500.00	$10,500.00	$890.00	$1,500.00	$750.00	

Mathematical Operations in Excel

Working with formulas and functions can become very complex; therefore, knowing Excel's standard format for performing calculations and the order in which they are performed with multiple operators helps to break down the process.

Table 2.1   Mathematical Operators Include

Addition (+)	Subtraction (−)	Multiplication (*)	Division (/)	Exponents (^)
=L1 + L2	M3-M2	J4*J7	Z1/Z4	X3 ^3
L1 and L2	Subtract M2 from M3	Multiplies J4 by J7	Divides Z1 by Z4	Cubes X3

Order of Operations

Formulas in Excel are calculated based on the **Order of Operation** which is a mathematical technique that provides a simplified step-by-step process for resolving a multiple operation equation.

1. Parentheses have priority—from left to right if more than one parentheses is used.
2. Exponential equations.
3. Multiplication and division—from left to right.
4. Addition and subtraction—from left to right.

Example: $= 6 + 9*(5\text{-}3)\text{-}3$

$1^{st} = 6 + 9*2\text{-}3$

$2^{nd} = 6 + 18\text{-}3$

$3^{rd} = 24\text{-}3$

$4^{th} = 21$

E2.6.1   Working with Excel Functions

Functions perform much of the same calculations as Formulas, but they offer a more efficient way to perform calculations. **Functions** can be identified by **reserved** words that are predefined in Excel. These predefined words perform specific actions based on the function's argument. The values enclosed in the parentheses make up the **Argument** for each function. **Note**: SUM is a **Function**. It is a **reserved** word used to perform a specific calculation in Excel.

Example: To add two cell values write: **= SUM(J2:M2)**.

Note: the colon **(:)** is used to separate the beginning cell address and the ending cell address, this is called a cell's **range** (i.e., the cells included in this range are (J2+K2+L2+M2).

Example: Let's recalculate Pham's Total Surcharge:

1. With the **Sum Function** still open,
2. **Delete** the contents from the previous examples for cells **I3** and **I4**.
    *   We will perform the same operation, but this time we will use a Function called **SUM** to perform the action.
3. Click in cell **I3** and type equal, **(=)**.
4. Type the Argument name, **SUM**
5. Type open parenthesis **(**
6. Type **E3:H3**
7. Close parenthesis **)**. **Note: Formula should not have spaces.**
8. Press the **enter** key on the keyboard. (Results are **$7370.00**).
9. Complete the **Total bill due** for the remaining guest.
10. **Continue** below to **save** work.

Note: Using the cell address rather than the actual numerical value gives you the power of having the worksheet update automatically when cell values change.

E2.7 Saving an Excel Workbook

When a workbook is created, you will need to save it initially in order to be able to retrieve it later. Excel offers two options for saving workbooks. The **Save** and **Save As** options.

Save As: this option should be used to initially save an Excel workbook. This option can also be used to make a copy of an original workbook or rename the workbook.

1. With the **sum function** still open.
2. Click the **file**: tab and select **Save As.**
3. Click **computer** then **brows**e to choose a file location, see *Figure 2.7*
4. Give the document a file name, **(MyExcel_E2).**
5. Click the **save** button. (Workbook is now saved).

Save: This option should be used after the workbook has been initially saved or given a file name. **Save** is located on the **Quick Access Toolbar,** as shown in Figure 2.8. As the workbook is edited and modified, **save** the document often so that changes made to the workbook are updated.

Note: Other options for saving include saving to the **Cloud** with Microsoft's **OneDrive**, saving to an external drive, or saving to your computer drive.

Figure 2.7   Save As

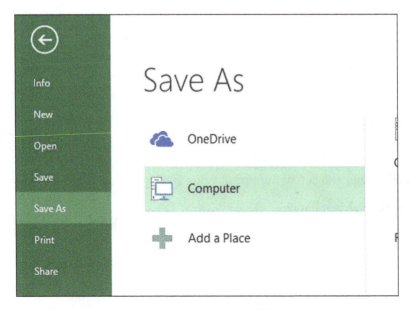

Figure 2.8   Save Button . . . Access Toolbar

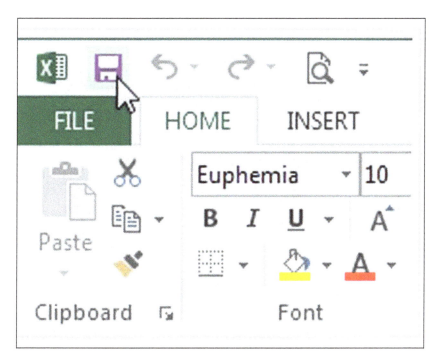

E2.7.1   Saving Other File Formats (Exporting a PDF)

All Excel 2013 file formats are saved as (**.XLSX**) by default; however, there are other file formats available for saving, including changing the file to an earlier version of Excel. Another file format that is available, is a Portable Document File, better known as a **PDF**.

The format for this file type will remain the same, and it will prevent changes from easily being made to the document. **PDFs** have many benefits crossing many platforms, thus making it available to anyone.

1. Choose a document to save in PDF format (an exercise worksheet such as the **sum function**).
2. Select the **File** tab.
3. Click the **Export** command from the navigation pane on the left. See Figure 2.9.
4. Select **Create a PDF/XPS Document** from the selection pane.
5. Click to **Create PDF/XPS.**
6. A **Publish as PDF or XPS** dialog box opens, notice the **Save as type**.
7. Select the location to export the file, then enter a **file name, as shown in Figure 2.10**
8. Click to **Publish.**

Figure 2.9   Export Command

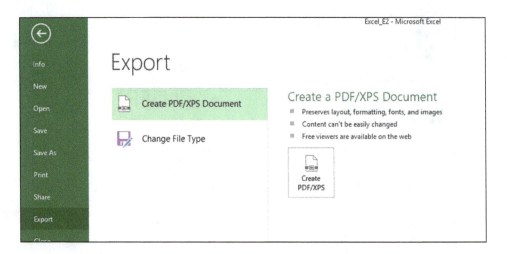

Figure 2.10   Publish PDF

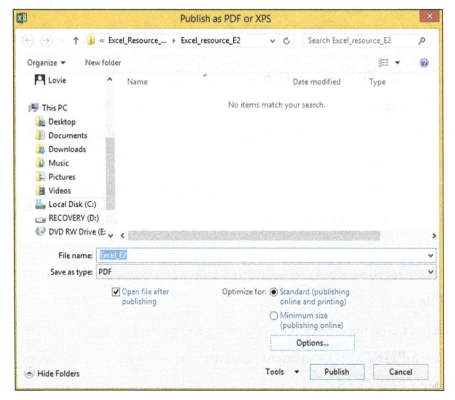

Note: Excel will automatically export the **active worksheet** by default if a selection is not made. For other worksheet options of exporting, view the **Options** selection button.

E2.7.2   Changing File Type (Other Exporting Options)

Excel offers other options to save and **Export** the workbook.

1. Select the **file** tab.

2. Click the **Export** tab, as shown in Figure 2.11

3. Select **Change File Type**, choose from the selections shown and follow the steps for the **Save As** feature.

4. Click **save** when finished. File will be saved in new format.

Figure 2.11   Change File Type

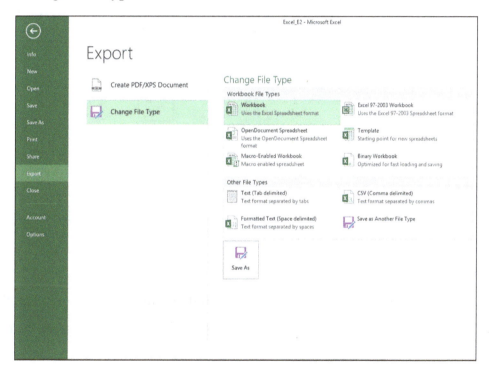

E2.8   Page Layout and Excel Printing Options

Excel has two page **Orientation** options for printing a document, **Portrait** and **Landscape**. These two formats have adjustable scaling options for printing a Workbook.

1. Click the **Page Layout** tab and click the down arrow of the **Orientation** command in the **Page Setup** group. See Figure 2.12.

2. Choose either (**Portrait** or **Landscape**) to change the document's page **Orientation**.

3. Document will immediately reflect the **Orientation** change.

Figure 2.12   Page Orientation

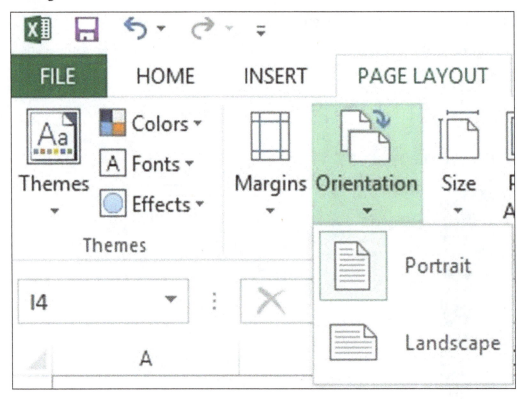

E2.8.1   Checking Page Margins

Setting the proper **margins** can help give your printed workbook an impressive look. The margin includes the blank space from the edge of the content on your worksheet outward to the edge of the page.

1. Make sure the **Sum Function** workbook **is** still open.

2. Click the **Page Layout** tab and select the down arrow of the **Margins** command in the **Page Setup** group, as shown in Figure 2.13.

3. Choose your **Margin** preference. (Settings will adjust immediately**).**

Figure 2.13   Page Setup

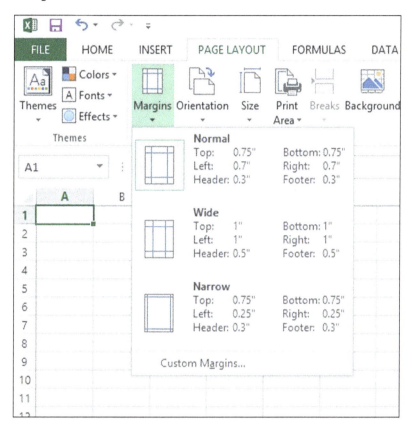

E2.8.2   Customized Margins

4. Select **Custom Margins** from the drop-down menu to view the **Page Setup** dialog box and adjust the settings to your preference, see Figure 2.14.

5. Click **OK**, when finished.

6. Workbook will adjust to the **Custom Margins** settings.

Figure 2.14   Margins

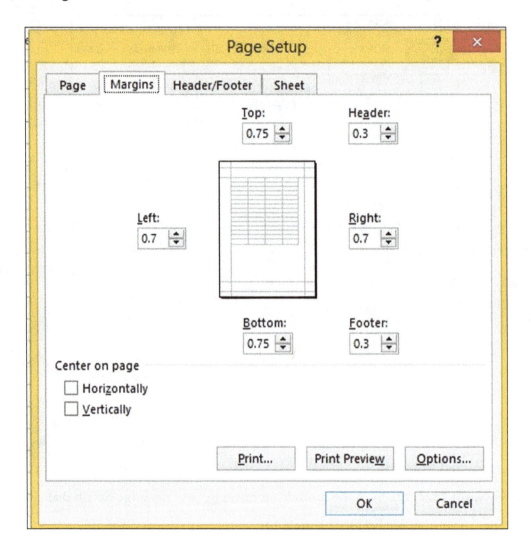

E2.8.3   Other Worksheet Printing Options

Setting a *specific* **Print area** for printing an **Excel** Worksheet.

1. Select the **sum function** worksheet.

2. Select cells **A1:D16,** as shown in Figure 2.15.

3. Click the **File** tab.

4. Select the **Print** command from the navigation pane on the left.

5. Click the down arrow for the **Settings** command to view the different ways to print the worksheet/workbook.

6. Choose the **Print Selection** to print only the **highlighted** section(s) of your **worksheet.** (Preview print selection on the right).

7. Click to **print** selection.

Figure 2.15   Selected Cells

	A	B	C	D
1		Dynasty Resort		
2	Guest F Name	Guest Last Name	# Days	Room Rate
3	Kim	Pham	7	$700.00
4	George	Gorman	7	$1,200.00
5	Mike	Davis	6	$1,500.00
6	Jan	Nelson	7	$1,500.00
7	Tim	Zoro	11	$2,700.00
8	Kate	Simmons	6	$750.00
9	Phia	Neeley	12	$2,000.00
10	Joyce	Neel	10	$2,000.00
11	Sally	Vanesse	8	$1,600.00
12	Eva	Forsberg	8	$1,600.00
13	Rose	Campbell	16	$5,000.00
14	Caroline	Greta	5	$700.00
15	Jamie	Roux	6	$800.00
16	Kaycee	LaSalle	20	$3,800.00

Step 5   Print Settings

E2.8.4   Repeating Rows

In order to have rows in your spreadsheet repeat for each printed page of your document, you would select the **Rows to Repeat**.

1. With the **sum function** open.

2. Click the **Page Layout** tab.

3. Select the **Print Titles** command in the **Page Setup** group. A **Page Setup** dialog box opens.

4. Position the insertion point in the field, **Rows to repeat at top.**

5. Type **[$1:$2].**

6. Click **ok**, and **Rows to repeat** will be included for each page of the worksheet. (**Note**: to preview and test the rows to repeat, cell content must extend beyond row 51 of your worksheet).

Hint: you may also use the collapse/expand command box, (to the far right of the rows to repeat at top) to select the cells from the spreadsheet and the cell address will automatically be inserted for you. See Figure 2.16.

Figure 2.16   Rows to Repeat

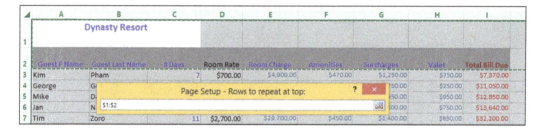

E2.8.5   Headers/Footers

Add a header and footer to your workbook to add some finishing touches, such as page numbering, and dates. **Excel** has several preset formats to choose from.

7. With the **sum function** still open,

8. Select the **Insert** tab and select the **Header & Footer** command from the down arrow of the **Text command** group. (**Note**: the worksheet now appears in **Page Layout** view).

9. The **Header/Footer** will open with the insertion point in the header/footer of the worksheet.

10. Click to select the header/footer *placeholder* and begin typing your name. (See Figure 2.17.)

❖ The **Header/Footer Tools** contextual tab opens with a list of commands that are available for modifying your **Header & Footer,** as shown in Figure 2.18.

11. To add or customize the **Footer**, select the **Go to Footer** command in the **Navigation** group of the **Design** tab of the **Header/Footer Tools** contextual tab screen and begin typing desired **Footer** content. (Changes will be visible immediately).

12. To return to **Normal** view, click outside of the **Header/Footer** placeholder and select **Normal** from the worksheet views (at the bottom of the Excel window). (**Hint**: you may also select the normal command from the **view** tab on the ribbon.)

Figure 2.17   Page Header/Footer

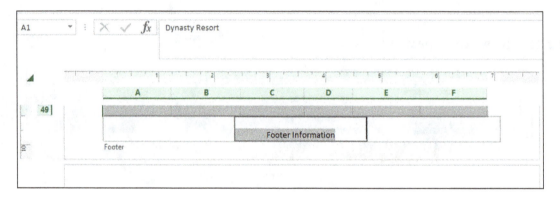

Figure 2.18   Header Contextual Tab

E2.9   Closing/Exiting Excel

To **close** the Excel workbook.

1. Click the **File** tab.
2. Select **Close** from the navigation pane on the left.
3. Current workbook will **close**.

❖   Alternately, you can click the **X** in the right corner of the screen to **exit** the workbook.

Section 3   Modifying an Excel Worksheet

[Student Resource Folder—(Excel_resource_E3)]

E3.1   Inserting Columns and Rows in a Worksheet

1. Open the **Excel_E3** workbook and select the **Columns** worksheet.

2. Select column **B** to insert a new column, as shown in Figure 3.1.

❖ Column headings are selected by including the **letter** above the column.

❖ Row headings are selected by including the **number** to the left of the row.

3. From the **Home** tab, click the **Insert** command that is located in the **Cells** group. **Note**: Columns all shift to the right, and the **new column** is **inserted** to the left of the selected cell, as shown in Figure 3.2. (**Note**: Rows will shift down below the **new** inserted **row**).

4. **Continue** to next section.

Figure 3.1   Selected Column

	A	B	C	D	E
1	Model	Rating	Condition	Cost	Division
2					
3	Toshiba Satel	5	Excellent	$249.99	SW
4	HP All-in-One	4	Good	$479.95	SE
5	Dell Opti-plex	5	Excellent	$89.95	NW
6	Dell Inspiron	2	Fair	$355.99	NE
7	Acer-Aspire	1	Poor	$159.99	SW
8	HP Pavilion	4	Excellent	$645.99	NE
9	HP Stream	3	Good	$329.75	SW
10					

B1 — Rating

Figure 3.2   New Inserted Column

	A	B	C
1	Model		Rating
2			
3	Toshiba Satelite		5
4	HP All-in-One		4
5	Dell Opti-plex		5
6	Dell Inspiron		2
7	Acer-Aspire		1
8	HP Pavilion		4
9	HP Stream		3

B1

E3.1.2   Deleting Columns and Rows in a Worksheet

Deleting columns will automatically cause the remaining columns in the worksheet to all shift to the left, as shown in Figure 3.3. However, when a row is deleted, the remaining data in the worksheet shift upward.

1. Select column **B** (the new inserted column) for deletion.

2. On the **Home** tab, select the **Delete** command in the **Cells** group.

Figure 3.3   Column Deleted

	A	B	C
	Model	Rating	Condition
1	Model	Rating	Condition
2			
3	Toshiba Satelite	5	Excellent
4	HP All-in-One	4	Good
5	Dell Opti-plex	5	Excellent
6	Dell Inspiron	2	Fair
7	Acer-Aspire	1	Poor
8	HP Pavilion	4	Excellent
9	HP Stream	3	Good

B1 — fx — Rating

E3.1.3   Moving Columns/Rows in a Worksheet

1. With the **columns** worksheet still open.

2. Select column **C** (to move).

3. Select the **Cut** command from the **Home** tab of the **Clipboard** group.

4. Next, select column **A** (to place the **moved** data).

5. From the **Home** tab, click the down-pointing arrow of the **Insert** command, in the **Cells** group.

6. Choose **Insert Cut Cells** from the drop-down menu. (**Column/row** will shift to reflect the move, as shown in Figure 3.4).

Step 3 Before move

| C1 | ▼ | : | ✕ ✓ *fx* | Condition |

	A	B	C
1	Model	Rating	Condition
2			
3	Toshiba Satelite	5	Excellent
4	HP All-in-One	4	Good
5	Dell Opti-plex	5	Excellent
6	Dell Inspiron	2	Fair
7	Acer-Aspire	1	Poor
8	HP Pavilion	4	Excellent
9	HP Stream	3	Good

Figure 3.4   After move

| A1 | ▼ | : | ✕ ✓ *fx* | Condition |

	A	B	C	D	E
1	Condition	Model	Rating	Cost	Division
2					
3	Excellent	Toshiba Satelite	5	$249.99	SW
4	Good	HP All-in-One	4	$479.95	SE
5	Excellent	Dell Opti-plex	5	$89.95	NW
6	Fair	Dell Inspiron	2	$355.99	NE
7	Poor	Acer-Aspire	1	$159.99	SW
8	Excellent	HP Pavilion	4	$645.99	NE
9	Good	HP Stream	3	$329.75	SW

E3.2   Wrapping Text

When the content in a cell is not displayed because of too much data, **Wrap Text** may be an effective option to apply. The height of a cell's row will automatically be adjusted to fit the cell's content.

1. With the **columns** worksheet still selected.

2. Select column **B,** as shown in Figure 3.5**.**

3. On the **Home** tab, click the **Wrap Text** command in the **Alignment** group. (Note the rows expand to display the wrapped text.)

Figure 3.5   Wrap Selected Column

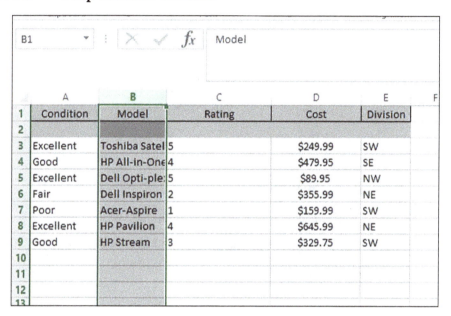

Step 3   Wrap Text Command

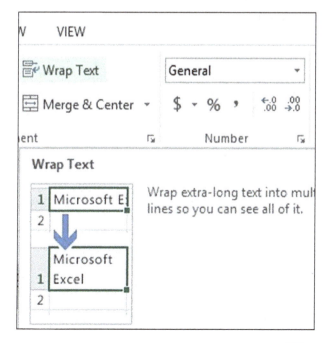

Adjusting Column and Row Width and Height

Manually adjusting the Column's width and the row's height is an option that can enhance the look of your worksheet. Increased spacing between columns and rows will effectively improve the flow of reading the content.

1. Open the **Pay** worksheet.
2. Position the pointer of the mouse in between the column boundaries of column **A** and column **B** until the pointer becomes a black double-headed arrow.
3. Left click and hold with the mouse to increase or decrease to the desired column's width or row's height. **Hint**: You may also double click the double-headed arrow to have the column/row automatically expand.

E3.3   Inserting/Deleting and Renaming Worksheets

By default, an Excel workbook opens with at least one worksheet included. Worksheets are sometimes referred to as tabs and they are labeled as **Sheet 1**, **Sheet 2**, and so forth. Sheets can be added or deleted as necessary and renamed or colored according to your preference.

1. With the **Excel_E3** workbook open,
2. Click the plus (**+**) sign at the bottom of the worksheet to add a **New Sheet**.
3. Right click the tab. Select **Rename** from the menu that pops up.
4. Type **Rep-Sales** for the new name.

Step 2   Add New Sheet

Step 4   Rename

Deleting Worksheets

1. Right click **Rep-Sales.**

2. Select **Delete** to remove the sheet from the workbook.

   ❖ **A Microsoft Excel warning box pops up, cautioning you that this action cannot be reversed, as shown in Figure 3.6**

3. **Save** changes.

Figure 3.6   Deleting Sheets

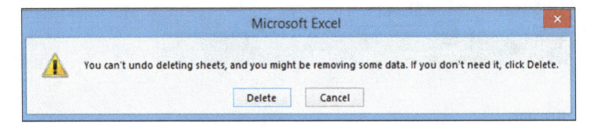

E3.4   Moving/Copying Worksheets

As the number of worksheets increase in your workbook, it may be necessary to organize the worksheets and rearrange the tab order for the best possible working results.

1. Right click the **flash-fill** worksheet.

2. Select **Move or Copy** from the menu that pops up.

   ❖ The **Move or Copy** dialog box opens, as shown in Figure 3.7.
   ❖ Worksheets can also be moved to other Excel workbooks however, the destination workbook must be open to\ complete this process.

3. Under the **before sheet** selection.

4. Select the **columns** worksheet so that the flash-fill worksheet will move in front.

5. Click **OK,** to close the **Move or Copy** dialog box. (The flash-fill sheet should now be in front of the columns worksheet).

Copying Worksheets

1. Right click the **pay** worksheet.

2. Select the **Move or Copy** command and select the pay worksheet.

3. Check the **create a copy** box at the bottom of the dialog box.

4. Click **OK**. Note that a copied worksheet automatically has an extension of **(2)** added to the original sheet name.

Figure 3.7   Move or Copy Sheets

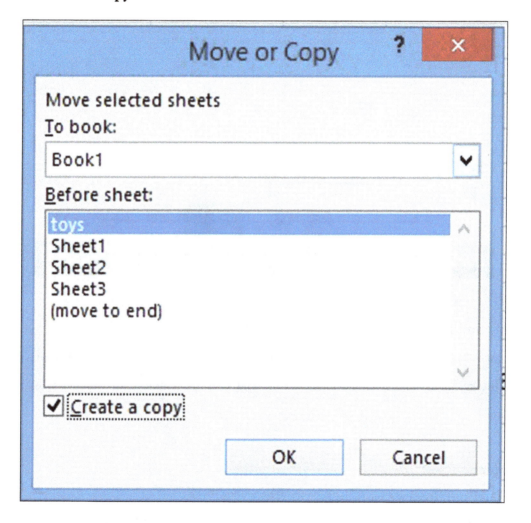

Step 4   Copied Sheets

E3.5   Finding and Replacing Data in a Worksheet

Searching for values and data can become very cumbersome especially, if the worksheet has large amounts of data. Excel makes it easy to find the information that you are looking for quicker with the **Find and Replace** feature.

Finding Content

1.   Select the **Find/Replace** worksheet.

2.   From the **Home** tab, click the **Find & Select** command, in the **Editing** group.

3.   Select **find** from the drop-down list; a **Find & Replace** dialog box will appear.

4.   Type *Video Tech*.

5.   Click **Find Next** to scroll through each occurrence of the term. (There are three instances of the phrase to be replaced).

Replacing the Content

1. Click the **Replace** tab.

2. Type *AV Tek* in the **Replace with** field, as shown in Figure 3.8.

3. Review the content to be replaced.

4. Click **Replace** for one instance to be replaced or click **Replace All** to replace every instance of the term.

5. Click **close** when you are finished. The dialog box will close.

6. **Save** and continue.

Figure 3.8   Find/Replace

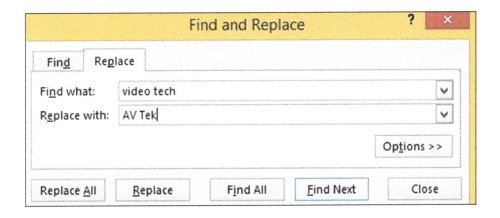

E3.6   Formatting Data in a Worksheet

By default, the **Font** for Excel is **Calibri** and the **font size** is set to 11 points. There are many other font colors and sizes to choose from.

1. With the **Find/Replace** worksheet still selected,

2. Select cell **A2.**

3. From the **Home** tab, select the down arrow next to the **Font** command in the **Font** group.

   ❖ Scroll down the list of fonts with your pointer.

   ❖ View the **Live Preview**, a featured preview of how your content will appear.

4. Select font type **Arial Black.**

5. Click the arrow next to the **Font Size** and change the **Font Size** to **14.**

   With **A2** still selected.

6. Select the down arrow for the **Font Color.**

7. Select **Black, Text 1.**

8. **Save** file and continue.

Step 3   Font Command

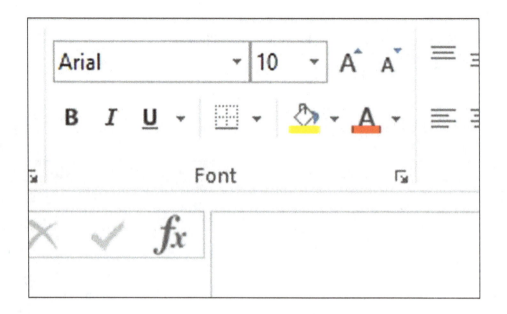

E3.6.1   Changing Text Alignment and Formatting Numeric Values

1. With the **Find/Replace** worksheet still selected.

2. Select the cell range **B5:B15.**

3. From the **Home** tab, click the **Center** command in the **Paragraph** group. The contents will be centered in the selected cells.

4. Select cell range **E5:E15.**

5. From the **Home** tab, select the **Increase Decimal** command in the **Number** group.

6. Notice, the cells reflect two decimal places with **E5:E15** still selected.

Step 5 Increase Decimal

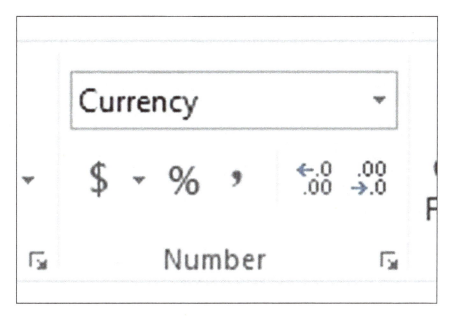

7. From the **Home** tab, click the down arrow for the **Number Format** command located in the **Number** group.

8. Select the **Currency** format.

   ❖ **Note the ($) symbol is now reflected in the check amounts.**

9. **Save** file and continue.

E3.6.2 Applying Format Painter (Fill Color)

The **Format Painter** copies the formatting of one cell to another. The **Format Painter** is a quick way to apply a consistent, professional look to your worksheet.

1. With the **Find/Replace** worksheet still selected,

2. Select cell **A2.**

3. From the **Home** tab, click the down arrow for the **Fill Color**command in the **Font** group.

4. Select the **Turquoise Accent 1 Color.**

   ❖ Notice the **Fill Colors** of the selected cells changed.

5. Select cell **A6:H6** and repeat step 4.

6. From the **Home** tab, left click once on the **Format Painter** command in the **Clipboard** group.

   ❖ Notice the pointer resembles a **Paint Brush.**

Step 6   Format Painter

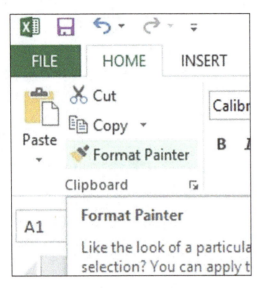

7. Brush across the cell range, **A8:H8** and every other row. (**Note**: Double click the format painter to toggle it on for continuous use).

    ❖ Note that the format was copied to the selected range of cells.
    ❖ Deselect the range by clicking outside of the range area.

8. **Save** worksheet and continue.

E3.7   Sorting Data in an Excel Worksheet

Sometimes the contents in a worksheet are much easier to analyze if it is organized properly. Excel offers a **Sort & Filter** feature for analyzing your data in **ascending** or **descending** order. Sorting can also be **customized** based on the content in the worksheet such as dates, values, or other information in the worksheet.

1. Select the **Sorting** worksheet.
2. Right click in cell **B2** to **Sort**).
3. Scroll down to the **Sort** command.
4. Choose the **A-Z Sort.** Notice the worksheet is **sorted** by last name, in order from A–Z, as shown in Figure 3.9.
5. **Save** and continue.

Figure 3.9   Sorted Data

E3.8   Filtering Data in Excel

Once data has been properly sorted and analyzed, applying a **Filter** makes it easier to extract only the needed information in your worksheet or report. (**Note**: When filtering, include the header titles for filtering to be most effective).

1. With the **Sorting** worksheet still selected.
2. Right click cell **C1.**

3. Point to the arrow next to the **Filter** command, then arrow over and choose the **Filter by Selected Cell's Value** (from the sub-menu that appears). **Note:** a drop-down arrow will appear in the header for each column.

  ❖ The drop-down allows you to apply other filters and select or search for specific data.

Applying a Number Filter Greater (>) than 1500.

4. Click the drop-down arrow in **C1**.

5. Point to the arrow next to the **Number Filters**.

6. Choose the **Greater Than** command from the sub-menu. (Notice a **Custom AutoFilter** dialog box opens).

7. In the **greater than** field type *1500*.

  ❖ View the new filtered data contents.

8. To remove **Filter**, click the **Data** tab.

9. Toggle the **Filter** command in the **Sort & Filter** group, as shown in Figure 3.10. (Note: the **Filter** is removed).

10. **Save** work and continue.

  ❖ **Note:** Filters are a temporary way of analyzing your data.

Figure 3.10   Filters

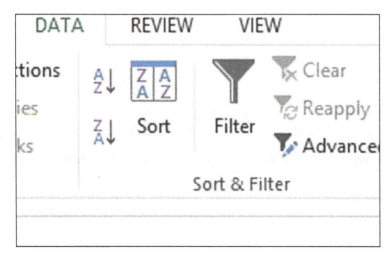

E3.9   Freezing Panes in a Worksheet

Freeze panes help to keep portions of your rows or columns visible on the screen as you scroll through the worksheet. This is effective for analyzing data in other parts of the worksheet.

1. With the **Sorting** worksheet still selected,
2. Select the first row. (**A1:C1**)
3. Select the **View** tab, click the down-pointing arrow for **Freeze Panes** in the **Windows** group.

Step 3   Freeze Panes

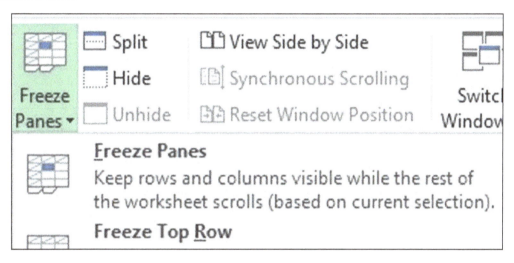

4. Select the **Freeze Top Row** command.
5. Scroll down vertically in the worksheet with the scroll bar, notice the **Top Row** is frozen.
6. To remove **Freeze Panes**, click the **Freeze Panes** command down arrow.
7. Select **Unfreeze Panes.**
8. **Save** work.

E3.10 Fill Handle

The **fill option** is used to fill adjacent cells with the same data or consecutive data. The **fill option** is different from copying because the contents are not placed on the clipboard. The fill option saves time, especially when there are numerous cells to fill.

1. Select the **Flash Fill** worksheet.

2. Select cell **[G2]** to copy. The **fill handle** will appear as a small **rectangle** at the bottom of the selected cell.

   ❖ The **fill handle** is used to fill the formula or contents to the adjacent cells.

3. Move the mouse toward the **fill handle** in **G2** until it changes to a plus (**+**) sign.

4. Left click, hold and drag the mouse (down) towards cell **G13**, and release the mouse.

5. Selected cells are filled.

6. **Save** and continue.

Step 2   Fill Handle

G2	▼ : ✕ ✓ *fx*	=F2/4				
	A	B	C	D	E	F	G

	Client	FName	LName	City	Contract Type	Contract Amt	Quarterly
2	M.Shawn	Mary		Baltimore	Instructor	4,000.00	1,000.00
3	J.Wells	Jim		Portland	Designer	30,000.00	
4	J.Meyers	Jan		San Diego	PM	15,000.00	
5	J.Grant	Jessica		Seattle	Script Reader	22,250.00	

E3.10.1   Flash Fill in a Worksheet

Excel 2013 has added a new feature called **Flash Fill**. This new feature automatically enters data into your worksheet by guessing from the pattern design in your worksheet.

1. Continue with the **Flash Fill** worksheet.

2. Select cell **C2.**

3. Type *Shawn*, the last name of the student as it appears in **A2**, and press the enter key.

4. Select cell **C3**, type *Wells* and press enter.

5. Notice a **Flash Fill** preview will appear when it has guessed the data pattern. (If the flash fill pattern doesn't appear, type the next name).

6. Select **enter** from the keyboard to accept the flash fill data.

7. The **Flash Fill** data will be added.

❖ To make adjustments to the **Flash Fill** options, click the arrow next to the **Flash Fill options** selection.

8. **Save** and close.

Filling Series

The **fill option** can also be used to fill **consecutive data** in a series such as the months of the year, dates, values, and times, as well as other patterns.

In the **fill series** worksheet, the cells in column **A** establishes the pattern for the series. View the **Auto fill** option drop-down menu that appears after the series has been filled. Point to the arrow, and the menu will expand and display a list of the different fill options that are available. Notice that the **Fill Series** is the default fill option.

1. Click the fill option handle in cell **A7** and fill the series (to the right); stop at **G7**.
2. Repeat steps for A8, A9, and A10.

E3.11 Proofing the Excel Worksheet (Spell Check)

Proofing a document before printing saves time and money. Excel's **spelling** features assist with checking the accuracy of your document.

1. Select the **Review** tab.
2. Choose the **Spelling** command in the **Proofing** group.
3. A **Spelling** dialog box opens, as shown in Figure 3.11.

❖ The spell checker will highlight words that are not found in the dictionary. You may choose to **ignore** the suggestions or accept the **change** in the worksheet. The **Options** button will allow you to **customize the dictionary** and make the necessary changes for how **Excel** proofs your document in the future.

4. Click **OK** once **spell check** is completed.

Figure 3.11   Spell Check

Step 4   Spell Check Complete

Section 4   Cell Addressing and More Functions

I.   Applying Relative and Absolute Cell Addressing

II. Applying the Insert Function

III. Creating PMT Functions

IV. Applying the IF Logical Function

V.   Applying the VLookup Function

[Student Resource Folder—(Excel_resource_E4)]

E4.1   Applying Relative and Absolute Cell Addressing

There are **two** types of cell references that define the cell address in Excel: **Relative** and **Absolute**. By default, when you copy and paste formulas, the cell address will change based on the row or column's **relative** position.

1. Open the **Functions** worksheet, click in cells **F3** and **F4.**

2. View the formula in the Formula Bar.

   Cell **F3**—relative address is: **=Average (B3:E3)**

   Cell **F4**—relative address is **=Average (B4:E4)**

The reference address of **F4** changed, based on the **Relative Address** of the **row** (**F3**) above it, (i.e., the rows are changing, [**3, 4**. . .]) as shown in Figure 4.1.

There are times when you do not want a cell's address to change, but instead you want it to remain **constant**. This is referred to as an **absolute** cell address. When there is an **Absolute Address** referenced in a cell, it is identified by a dollar (**$**) symbol. The (**$**) symbol usually precedes the column letter and or the row number, and it means that the cell address will remain unchanged at all times.

1. With the **Functions** worksheet open,

   ❖ You will add **Bonus points** to each student's **Total Test Grade** to calculate their **Total Test Points.**

   ❖ Notice the cell address for the **Bonus points** is an **Absolute cell address.**

2. Click in cell **G3, as** shown in Figure 4.2.

3. Type the formula, **=F3+G16** and press the enter key. (Results =89.8). Use auto fill to complete the remaining Student's Total Test Points.

4. **Save** work.

   ❖ Notice the **$** symbol in front of the column and in front of the row.

   ❖ This shows the cell's **absolute address** for the **bonus points**.

Note: By giving the cell's **absolute address**, you can change the value of the **bonus points** any time, and the grades will automatically be updated.

Figure 4.1   Relative Address

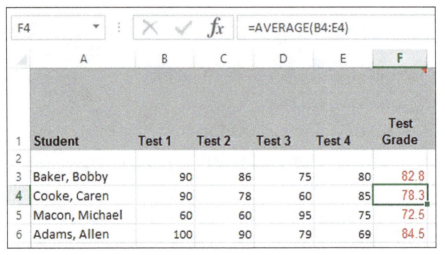

Figure 4.2   Absolute Address

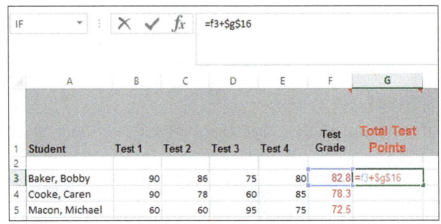

E4.2   Applying the Insert Function

The **Insert Function** allows you to search for functions based on Excel's **reserved** key words. There are many functions to choose from such as Financial Functions, Statistical Functions, Date Functions, Logical Functions, and several others. In the exercise below, we will insert the **Statistical Function, Count**.

1. With the **Functions** worksheet open,

2. Click in cell **B19.**

3. Click the **Insert Function** button, located on the **Formula Bar**. The **Insert Function** dialog box opens. Notice Excel inserts an equal, (**=**) sign into the cell.

Step 3   Insert Function

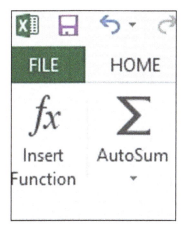

4. Type **Max** in the **Search for a function** text box.

5. Then select **Max** from the **select a function** list.

6. Click **OK**.

7. The **Function Arguments** dialog box opens.

8. Select the **Number 1** field.

9. Verify that the cell address range is **:B3:B12.** Make the adjustments, if needed.

10. Click **OK** when finished.

❖ Notice answer appears in cell **B19.**

❖ View formula in **Formula Bar.**

11. **Save** and **close.**

E4.3   Creating Payment Functions

Excel's **PMT** function is used to calculate loan payments based on an interest rate and payments that are constant. In this example you will use the **Insert Function** to determine which investor has the best possible offer for *BJ's Custom Tiling* to accept.

The argument for the PMT function is: PMT(rate, nper, pv, [fv], [type])

Note: an argument is the information needed to calculate and it is usually enclosed in parentheses.

- Rate (required) – The interest rate for the loan.
- Nper (required) – The total number of payments for the loan.
- Pv (required) – The present value, or principal.
- Fv (optional) – The future value of a loan.
- Type (optional) – The number (0) or (1) indicating when payments are due.

1. Open **Ex-PMT worksheet.**
2. Click in cell **B7.**
3. Click the **Insert Function** command on the **Formula Bar.**
4. Type *PMT* in the **search for a function** field and click **Go,** as shown in Figure 4.3.
5. Select **PMT** from the **select a function** category listing.
6. Click **OK.**
7. The **Function Arguments** dialog box opens, as shown in Figure 4.4.

Figure 4.3   PMT Function

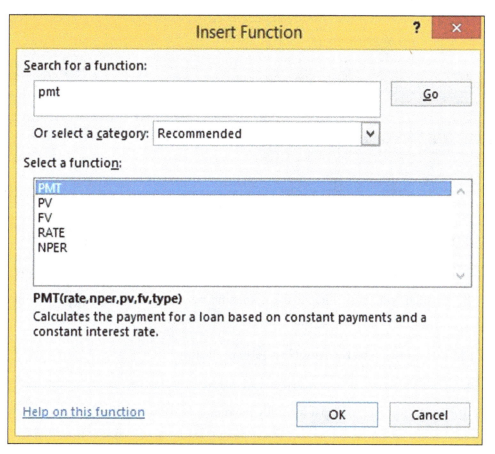

8. With the insertion point in the rate field, type **B3/12**

    ❖ Dividing the annual interest rate by 12 gives the monthly interest rate for the loan (**Note**: 12 is the number of months in a year).

9. Next, click in the **Nper** field and type **B4 *12**

    ❖ Multiplying by 12 gives the actual number of payments to be made on the loan.

10. Click in the **PV** field, type **B5** and click **OK.**

    ❖ Note: **PV** represents the principal value that is being borrowed.
    ❖ Loan payments are displayed in red.

Figure 4.4   Function Argument

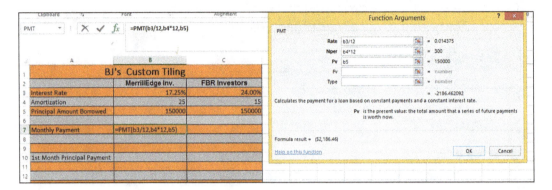

11. Select cell **B10** and click the **Insert Function** command on the **Formula Bar**.

12. Type *PPMT* in the **search for a function** field of the **Insert Function** dialog box. Note: (PPMT) returns the payment on the principal for a specific period with constant payments and a constant interest rate.

13. Select **PPMT** from the **select a function** category listing.

14. Click **OK**.

15. Type the following for the principal monthly payment, as shown in Table 4–1.

Table 4–1   Principal Monthly Payment

Rate	B3/12		Nper	B4*12
Per	1		PV	B5

Rate	B3/12	Nper	B4*12
Per	1	PV	B5[end table]

Per = 1 is the 1ˢᵗ months principal. Per must be a range from 1 to **Nper**. It is the calculation for the principal payment for a specific period of time. **Hint:** to calculate the final principal payment, (**Per = Nper.**)

16. Select cell **B14.**

17. Type **=B4*12*B7.**

18. Press **enter** from the keyboard**.**

19. **Save** and close**.**

Note: complete the PMT and PPMT for FBR Investors.

- Interest rate is yearly.

- Amortization is the years.

- Monthly payment includes principal and interest.

E4.4   Applying the IF Logical Function

The **IF Function** is a logical test that returns a value, based on a condition. A value is returned if a condition is **true**, and a value is returned if a condition is **false**. The syntax of an **IF Function** is shown below in Table 4–2:

Table 4–2   IF (logical test, value_if_true, value_if_false)

If Logical Function	Result
=IF(D3>85,D3+E12, D3	If the value in D3 is greater than 85, Add the number in E12 to the number in D3, else return the value in D3.
=IF(F7>12,"Reorder", "Discontinue")	If the value in F7 is greater than 12, "Reorder", else "Discontinue".

1. Open the *Awards* worksheet; click in cell **F4.**

2. Click the **Insert Function** command on the Formula Bar**.**

3. Type **IF,** in the **search for a function** field and click **Go.**

4. Select **IF** from the **select a function** category listing.

5. Click **OK.**

6. This opens the **Function Arguments** dialog box, as shown in Figure 4.5.

7. With the insertion point in the **Logical test** field.

8. Type **E4 > 250**, press the **tab** key on the keyboard.

9. Type **Outstanding** and press tab.

10. Type **Good.**

11. Click **OK** to close the **Function Arguments** dialog box.

12. Use the **fill function** to fill the remaining cells.

13. **Save** and close.

❖ Quotation marks are not needed around the words **Outstanding** and **Good** because the **Insert Function** is programmed to add the quotation marks for you.

Figure 4.5   Logical Function

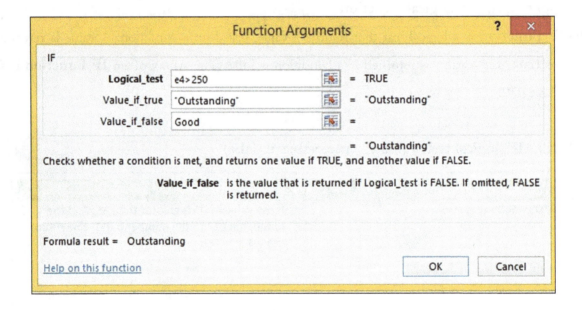

E4.5   Applying the VLookup Function

The **VLookup** function is used quite often when you are searching for things in a table or a range by row. There are three types of lookup functions, Vlookup, Hlookup, and Lookup. Vlookups work with vertical tables. Hlookups work with horizontal tables, and Lookup works with either.

The key to the Vlookup is to display the value that you want to look up on the left of the value that you want to have return. There are four arguments for the Vlookup with one of them being optional. The syntax for the Vlookup is as follows:

VLookup (lookup value, table array, col index num, [range lookup]). See Table 4-3 for the function arguments.

Table 4–3   Vlookup Argument Description

Argument	Description
Lookup value	Required; and value must be in the first column of the range of cells
Table array	Required; and the first column in the cell range must contain the lookup value and the cell range needs to include the return value
Col index num	Required; column number in order from left to right (beginning with 1). False searches for the exact value in the first column. True searches for the closes value. **Note**: Column must be sorted numerically or alphabetically.
Range lookup	Optional;

In the following exercise we will apply the Vlookup Function to get the names of Niki's Employee's by looking up their Employee ID#.

1. Open **Niki's** worksheet; click in cell **G5.**
2. Click the **Insert Function** command on the Formula Bar**.**
3. Type **VLookup** in the **search for a function** field and click **Go.**
4. Select **VLookup** from the **select a function** category listing.
5. Click **OK**.
6. This opens the **Function Arguments** dialog box.
7. With the insertion point in the **Lookup_value** field. See Figure 4.4
8. Type **A5** in the **Lookup value** field and press the **tab** key on the keyboard.
9. Type **J16:K23** in the **Table_array** field, and type **2** in the **Col_index_num** field.
10. Click **OK**, to close the **Function Arguments** dialog box. (Use the **fill function** to fill the remaining cells).
11. **Save** and close.

Figure 4.4   Function Arguments

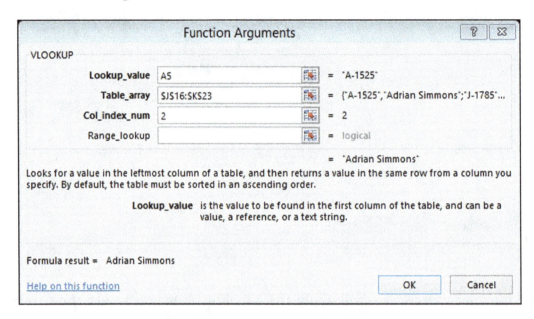

Note: the lookup value must be in the first column of the table array, and it must be sorted numerically, or alphabetically for this to work properly.

Section 5   Charts and Other Advanced Features

I.   **Creating a Column Chart**

II.   **Modifying Column Charts**

III. **Working with 3-D Pie Charts**

IV.   **Creating Sparklines in Excel**

V.   **Conditional Formatting**

VI.   **Protecting an Excel Workbook**

[Student Resource Folder—(Excel_resource_E5)]

Visually displaying numerical data with charts helps give others a graphical view of your worksheet data and provides a better understanding of the information being presented.

Charts vary in many different types such as column, pie, bar, and line. Charts can be inserted into the worksheet with the data included or inserted separately, displaying only the charts and graphs. Excel's new feature provides suggestions and recommendations to assist you in choosing the best possible chart for your data.

E5.1   Creating a Column Chart

1. Open the **Avon Sales** worksheet.

2. Select cells **A4:A10** to include in chart.

3. Next, select and hold the **Ctrl** key (simultaneously) on the keyboard while you select cells **C4:F10**. Once all cells are selected and highlighted, release mouse and the **Ctrl** key, as shown in Figure 5.1.

4. Click the **Insert** tab. Choose the chart type by clicking the down arrow for **Insert Column Chart** command from the **Charts** group.

5. Select **3-D Clustered Column,** (this column lets you compare values) as shown in Figure 5.2.

6. The **chart** is inserted into the worksheet. (Click in any empty cell to deselect chart selection).

❖ Notice that the **Chart Tools** contextual tab opens. Modifications can be made to the chart's **Design** and **Format** with this tab selection.

Figure 5.1   Selected Range

	Rep	Sales	January	February	March	April
4	J.Azevedo	6	$1,000.00	$1,950.00	$2,500.00	$2,900.00
5	A.Gomez	6	$800.00	$1,400.00	$1,650.00	$1,400.00
6	T. Paris	8	$2,500.00	$1,300.00	$1,900.00	$1,325.00
7	T. Williams	8	$1,000.00	$890.00	$1,500.00	$1,450.00
8	E. Locke	6	$900.00	$1,795.00	$890.00	$1,500.00
9	Marchant	14	$2,400.00	$2,100.00	$1,750.00	$1,650.00
10	S. Millian	8	$1,300.00	$1,795.00	$1,500.00	$1,795.00

Figure 5.2   3-D Clustered Column

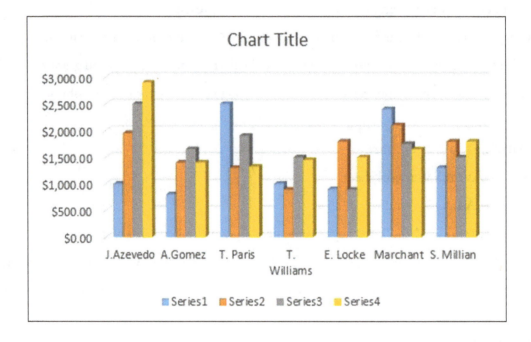

E5.2   Modifying Column Charts

1. With the worksheet **Avon Sales** still open.

2. Select the chart.

3. Triple click inside the **Chart's Title** to edit the **title**, type **Avon Commission.**

4. Select the **Design** tab of the **Chart Tools** contextual tab.

5. Click the **Quick Layout** down arrow in the **Chart Layouts** group; select **Layout 3.**

❖ To make modifications to the chart, make sure the chart is selected.

6. With the chart still selected, click the **Select Data** command in the **Data** group of the **Chart Tools** contextual tab to edit the **series**. (Select series 1, click **edit**, and rename to January; repeat for the remaining legend series).

7. Click on the **Design** tab of the **Chart Tools** contextual tab menu and select the **Move Chart** command in the **Location** group.

8. Select **New Sheet** from the **Move Chart** dialog box.

9. Click in the **New Sheet** field to name the chart, **Avon**.

10. Click **OK** when finished. Chart will be displayed in a **New Sheet**.

11. **Save**.

Step 6   Edit Series

E5.3   Working with 3-D Pie Charts

1. With **Avon Sales** worksheet selected.

2. Select cells **A4:A10.**

3. Next, select and hold the **Ctrl** key on the keyboard while you select cells **F4:F10**. Once all cells are selected and highlighted, release the mouse and the **Ctrl** key.

4. Click the **Insert** tab**.** Click the down arrow for the **Insert Pie** or **Doughnut Chart** command from the **Charts** group.

5. Select **3-D Pie**.

6. With the **Pie Chart** selected, choose **Style 8** from the **Chart Styles** group of the **Chart Tools Design** contextual tab.

7. Select the chart title and type *April Commission*.

8. Right click on the **Pie.** A sub-menu will pop up.

9. Select **Format Data Labels**. Under the **Label Options**, make sure **Category Name** and **Value** boxes are checked, as shown in Figure 5.3.

10. Right click on the **pie** and choose **3-D Rotation** from the sub-menu.

11. Make the **X** rotation = 10°, Y rotation = **30°** and **Perspective** = **15°**, as shown in Figure 5.4.

12. **Close** the **Format Chart** task pane when finished.

13. **Move** chart to a new sheet and title the chart *April*.

14. **Save** work**.**

Figure 5.3   Format Data Labels

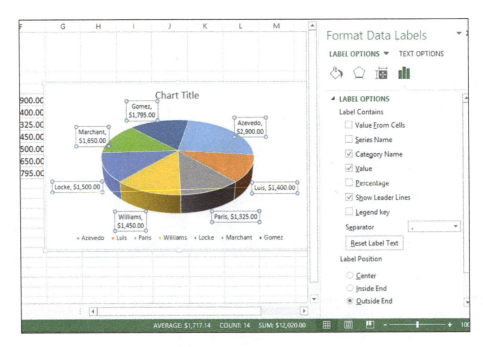

Figure 5.4   3-D Rotation

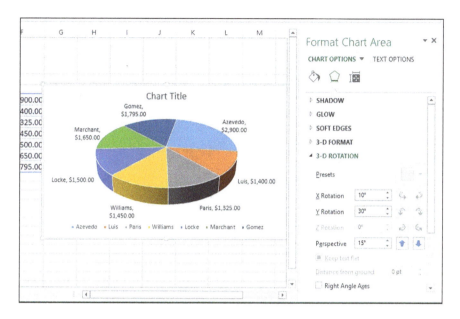

E5.4   Creating Sparklines in Excel

Sparklines are small charts that appear within a cell of your worksheet. These Sparklines help analyze your data by previewing the trends that your numerical data provide.

When you create a chart, it gives you the overall big picture of your data. However, Sparklines allow you to view your data in smaller increments. Sparklines provide a visual of your data from a different perspective for analyzing. There are three types of Sparklines: **Line**, **Column**, and **Win/Loss**.

1. With the **Avon Sales** worksheet still open, select cells **C4:F4** for the **data range.**
2. Click the **Insert** tab; then click the **Line** command in the **Sparkline's** group. A **Create Sparkline** dialog box will open.
3. Click in the field **Location range** and type **G4.**
4. Click **OK.**
5. A **Sparkline** will appear in the cell.
6. Apply the **fill handle** to create the remaining Sparklines. The trend shows the changes in each Rep's sales.
7. **Save** and continue.

❖ Click on the **Design** tab of the **Sparkline Tools** contextual tab to modify.

Step 3   Create Sparklines

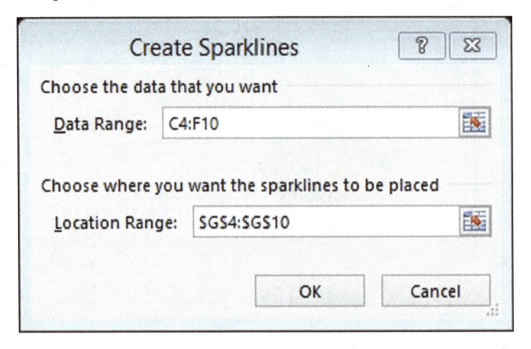

Step 5   Sparkline Results

Rep	Sales	January	February	March	April	Total Sales	
J.Azevedo	6	$1,000.00	$1,950.00	$2,500.00	$2,900.00	$8,350.00	
A.Gomez	6	$800.00	$1,400.00	$1,650.00	$1,400.00	$5,250.00	
T. Paris	8	$2,500.00	$1,300.00	$1,900.00	$1,325.00	$7,025.00	
T. Williams	8	$1,000.00	$890.00	$1,500.00	$1,450.00	$4,840.00	
E. Locke	6	$900.00	$1,795.00	$890.00	$1,500.00	$5,085.00	
Marchant	14	$2,400.00	$2,100.00	$1,750.00	$1,650.00	$7,900.00	
S. Millian	8	$1,300.00	$1,795.00	$1,500.00	$1,795.00	$6,390.00	

E5.5   Conditional Formatting

Conditional formatting allows you to visualize your data by applying a color format scheme that will help you view the trends and patterns for analyzation.

1. With the **Avon Sales** worksheet open, select cell range **C4:F10**.

2. From the **Home** tab, select the **Conditional Formatting** down arrow command in the **Styles** group.

3. Select **Greater Than** from the **Highlight Cells Rules** category, as shown in Figure 5.5.

4. A **Greater Than** dialog box opens. Type *1850* in the **Format cells that are Greater Than** field, as shown in Figure 5.6.

5. Pull the down arrow of the **with** field and select the **Light Red Fill With Dark Red Text**. (Cells will display **conditional formatting**).

6. Click **OK.**

❖ Deselect cells by clicking away from the highlighted cell range.

7. To **clear formatting**, select the **Conditional Formatting** down arrow command and select **Clear Rules.**

8. **Save** and close.

Figure 5.5   Conditional Fomatting

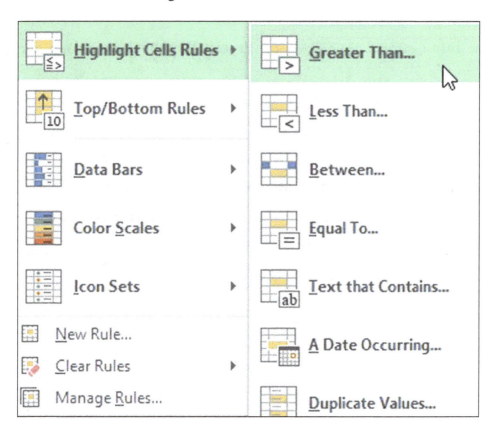

Figure 5.6   Greater Than Formatting

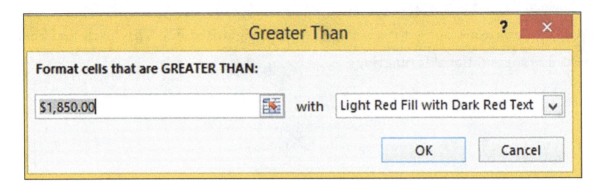

E5.6   Protecting an Excel Workbook

Excel offers protection for working on documents that may be confidential or to ensure that only authorized users have access.

1. Click the **File** tab.

2. From the **Info** navigation pane, select the **Protect Workbook** drop-down arrow, as shown in Figure 5.7.

3. Choose **Encrypt with Password** from the selection.

4. Notice an **Encrypt Document** dialog box opens, prompting you to enter a password, as shown in Figure 5.8.

5. After a password has been entered, a **Confirm Password** dialog box opens. (**Note**: the workbook is now password protected, and a password is required to open the workbook).

6. Click **OK**.

Figure 5.7   Protect Workbook

Figure 5.8   Encrypting Document

Integrating Office Applications

Integrating and Linking data across Microsoft Office applications is a common task. When linking data from an Excel spreadsheet to an Access database, updates can only be made from the source application. This would be an advantage for sharing data and information with those who are not as familiar with Access and prefer to continue maintaining data in an Excel spreadsheet format.

Integrating Programs (Access, Excel, Word)

    I.   Link/Embed an Excel Chart to Word

    II.   Copy and Paste a Word Table into an Excel Worksheet

    III. Link Data between an Excel and an Access

    IV. Edit Linked Data

[Student Resource File—Int_3

Int-1.1   Link/Embed an Excel Chart to Word

1. Open **NewReflection.xlsx.**
2. Open a **blank** Word document**.**
3. Select the **Veggies** spreadsheet and click the **Home** tab.
4. Select the **Ranking** chart in the spreadsheet and click the **copy** command in the **Clipboard** group.
5. Next, select the Word document and click the down-pointing arrow for the **paste** command**.**
6. Select the option, **Keep the source formatting and Embed Workbook.**
7. **Save** work as **My_NewReflection_Int** and **close**.

Note: Embedded objects are not automatically updated. Linked objects are updated.

Int-1.2   Copy and Paste a Word Table into an Excel Worksheet

1. Open **Timeline.docx**.
2. Open a **blank** spreadsheet in Excel.
3. With the **Timeline** document selected in **Word**, select the table and click the **copy** command in the **Clipboard** group of the **Home** tab.
4. Select the **Excel** spreadsheet and click inside cell **A1**.
5. Click the down-pointing arrow for the **paste** command and select a paste option.
6. **Save** work as **My_Timeline_Int** and **close**.

Int-1.3   Link Data between an Excel and Access

1. Open the **Faculty** database.

2. Click the **External Data** tab, as shown in Figure 1.

3. Select the **Excel** command in the **Import & Link** group. A **Get External Data-Excel Spreadsheet** dialog box opens.

4. Select the **Browse** button to locate the Excel source file, **Linking.xlsx**, in the student resource folder, as shown in Figure 2.

5. Select the **Linking.xlsx** workbook.

6. Click **open**.

Figure 1   Import & Link

Figure 2   Browse Files

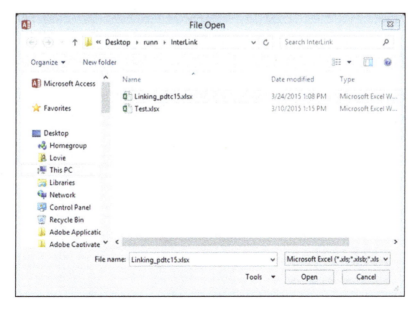

7. Check the **Link to the data source by creating a linked table** button, as shown in Figure 3.

8. Click **OK**. A **link spreadsheet wizard** dialog box opens; select the **Contractors** worksheet.

9. Click **next**.

10. Check the box **First Row Contains Column Headings.**

11. Click **next.**

12. Click **finish. (The Link Spreadsheet Wizard)** will confirm the link.

13. Click **OK**.

Figure 3   Linking Data Source

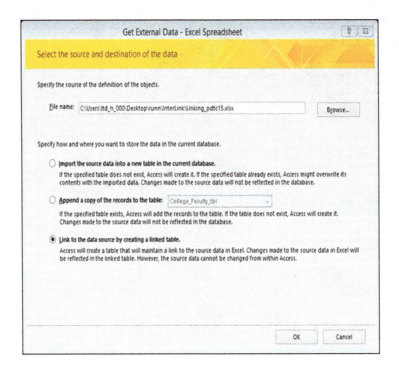

Hint—To Import an Excel Spreadsheet into Access without linking it, select the **Import the source data into a new table in the current database** button.

Step 8 Linking Wizard

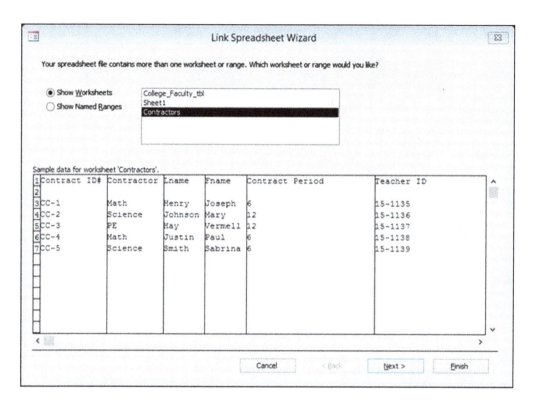

14. Notice: the linked table in Access has an Excel icon with a blue arrow next to it confirming that the table has been linked. See Figure 4.

15. Open the contractors table in Access to view the data. (**Note**: Changes cannot be made to the **linked** table in Access).

16. **Continue**.

Figure 4   Linking Table

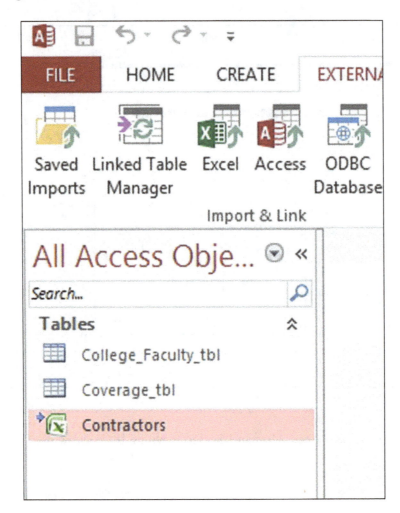

Int-1.4   Edit Linked Data

As we mentioned in the previous section, data can be linked with other Office applications, but changes can only be made from the source file. With the linked table **Contractors** closed in Access, we will make changes to the source file.

1. Open the Excel file **Linking.xlsx**.

2. Select the **contractors** worksheet. (**Notice** row two is empty).

3. Select row **two**, as shown in Figure 5.

4. Click the **Delete** command in the **Cells** group of the **Home** tab.

Figure 5   **Editing Linked Data**

	A	B	C	D	E	F
1	Contract ID#	Contractor	Lname	Fname	Contract Period	Teacher ID
2						
3	CC-1	Math	Henry	Joseph	6	15-1135
4	CC-2	Science	Johnson	Mary	12	15-1136
5	CC-3	PE	Hay	Vermell	12	15-1137
6	CC-4	Math	Justin	Paul	6	15-1138
7	CC-5	Science	Smith	Sabrina	6	15-1139
8						

5. Notice the rows all move up; see Figure 6.

6. Change the Contractor for Contract ID# CC-3 from PE to Philosophy.

7. Open the Access **linked** table, **contractors**. Notice the changes made in the Excel worksheet are reflected in the table in Access, as shown in Figure 7.

8. **Close** the workbook.

9. **Close** the Access database.

Figure 6   **Source Data Updated**

	A	B	C	D	E	F
1	Contract ID#	Contractor	Lname	Fname	Contract Period	Teacher ID
2	CC-1	Math	Henry	Joseph	6	15-1135
3	CC-2	Science	Johnson	Mary	12	15-1136
4	CC-3	PE	Hay	Vermell	12	15-1137
5	CC-4	Math	Justin	Paul	6	15-1138
6	CC-5	Science	Smith	Sabrina	6	15-1139
7						

Figure 7   Linked Data Updated

Contract ID#	Contractor	Lname	Fname	Contract Per	Teacher ID
CC-1	Math	Henry	Joseph	6	15-1135
CC-2	Science	Johnson	Mary	12	15-1136
CC-3	Philosophy	Hay	Vermell	12	15-1137
CC-4	Math	Justin	Paul	6	15-1138
CC-5	Science	Smith	Sabrina	6	15-1139

Index

Excel 2013

Knowledge and Skill Assessment

E1   Knowledge Check

1. The name box displays the _____ cell address.

2. The _____ _____ indicates where the next character appears in the document.

3. The _____ _____ displays the cells data.

4. Select the _____ tab to open a blank workbook.

5. The _____ gives you access to all of Excel's tasks and commands.

6. Click the _____ button to minimize the screen.

7. The _____ _____ are ways of viewing a workbook.

E2   Knowledge Check

1. When a cell is active, the _____ _____ will appear in the name box.

2. Click _____ to remove cell content.

3. _____ in Excel are based on the Order of Operation.

4. When there is multiplication and division in a formula, Excel performs the operation from _____ to _____.

5. Functions perform much of the same calculations as formulas, but functions are identified by _____ _____.

6. Saving an Excel workbook in a _____ format prevents changes from easily being made to the workbook and the workbook format remains the same.

7. The _____ _____ tab gives access to the Margins command.

E3.   Knowledge Check

1. **Columns** all shift to the _____ after a **new column** is **inserted** to the _____ of the selected cell.

2. **Rows** will shift _____ below the **new** inserted **row.**

3. When a column is deleted, the remaining data all shift to the _____.

4. The **cut** command is in the _____ group on the **Home** tab.

5. The copy command places items on the _____.

6. Excel makes it easy to find the information in a document with the _____ _____ command feature.

7. The ____ _____ command copies the formatting of one cell to another.

E4.   Knowledge Check

1. A cell's address that is constant and does not change is called the _____ _____, and the _____ symbol identifies it.

2. The _____ _____ command is located on the **Formula Bar.**

3. The _____ **Function** is a logical test that returns a value based on a condition.

4. The _____ function is used to calculate loan payments that are based on interest and consistent payments.

5. The **IF Function** returns a value if the condition is _____ and also if the condition is _____.

6. With **relative addressing** the _____ or the _____ may change.

7. The Insert Function command inserts the _____ into a cell once it is selected.

E5.   Knowledge Check

1. Click the _____ tab to view the Charts group.

2. The _____ _____ _____ command lets you insert a Clustered Chart into the workbook.

3. Modifying a chart can be done with the _____ _____ contextual tab selected.

4. The _____ _____ command allows you to move the chart to a new sheet in the workbook.

5. Modifications to the Chart styles can be done in the _____ tab of Chart Tools contextual tab.

6. _____ shows an analysis of your data by displaying small, mini charts within the cell of your worksheet.

7. _____ _____ shows a visual display of your data with a color scheme format.

Skill Assessments—1 and 2

Modify an Excel Workbook, Perform Calculations, Create a PDF
Student Resource Folder—(Assessment_E2)

1. Open the **Excel_SA_2** Workbook and select the **Movie** Worksheet.
2. Add the additional Movie Theater information below to the spreadsheet.

Movie Theater Information

Movie Theater	Pricing	Adults
Foxx Cinemas	$16.50	10
Park Place Cinemas	$13.95	6
Showtime Cinemas	$18.50	13

3. Calculate the **cost** for the adult tickets at each movie theater.
4. Insert a **Header/Footer** with your name and the date.
5. Create a **PDF** for the active sheet.
6. **Save** and **close** workbook.

Skill Assessment 3

Modify a Worksheet, Wrap Text, Insert Column, Insert Function, Sort, Find and Replace
Student Resource Folder—(Assessment_E3)

1. Open the **Excel_SA_3** workbook and select the **Invoice** worksheet.
2. Insert a new column between **B** and **C**. Label the new column **late fee.**
3. Add a fee of **.10%** for each unpaid invoice.
4. **Find** focus study and **Replace** with Focus Group.
5. **Wrap text** in column **A.**
6. **Save** and **exit.**

Skill Assessment 4

Using Functions, logical function, Vlookup, Absolute Function, the Insert Function

(Student Resource Folder—(Assessment_E4)

1. Open the **Excel_SA_4** workbook and select **J.R. Cars** worksheet.
2. Create a logical function to calculate the **Annual Bonus** for J.R. Sales Associates. The annual bonus is awarded based on a percentage of the Associate's Years of Service.
3. **Create a Vlookup function** to display the Sales Associate's name, (in cell **J8**) by looking up the Sales Associate's ID number.
4. Apply the **Sum Function** to calculate the **Total Annual Bonus** for all Associates and return the value in cell **C20**.
5. Format to **($)**, Currency.
6. **Save** and **close**.

Skill Assessment 5

Create Column Chart, Pie Chart, Apply the Absolute Function, Create Sparklines, Conditional Formatting

Student Resource Folder—(Assessment_E5)

1. Open the **Excel_SA_5** workbook and select **HAS Realty** worksheet.
2. Calculate the Realtor's Commission**.**
3. Create a **Clustered Column Chart** in a new sheet, labeled **July Sales,** that displays the Realtors *and* the Selling Price**.**
4. Title the chart appropriately. Choose appropriate layout and style modifications that will make the chart easy to understand.
5. Create a **3-D pie chart** that displays the Realtors and the Commission. Include a chart title and choose appropriate modifications.
6. Create **Sparklines** that display the Pricing Variance.
7. Apply **Conditional Formatting** for three different pricing amounts. Determine the formatting colors and amounts.
8. **Save** and **exit**.

Answer Key

E1.   Answer

1. Active

2. Insertion point

3. Formula Bar

4. File

5. Ribbon

6. Minimize

7. Workbook views

E2.   Answer

1. Cell address

2. Delete

3. Formulas

4. Left, right

5. Reserved words

6. PDF

7. Page Layout

E3.   Answer

1. Right, left

2. Down

3. Left

4. Clipboard

5. Clipboard

6. Find/Replace

7. Format Painter

E4.   Answer

1. Absolute address, $
2. Insert function
3. IF
4. PMT,
5. True, False
6. Row, Column
7. Equal sign, (=)

E5.   Answer

1. Insert
2. Insert Column Chart
3. Chart Tools
4. Move Chart
5. Design
6. Sparklines
7. Conditional Formatting

Access 2013

Access is a software application that is designed to retrieve, modify, or maintain related information in a database format. The information received is stored in objects that make up the structure of the database. The structure of the design of the database objects is to make information relational through the collection of data that is stored in related tables.

This tutorial will not only help to improve your skills, knowledge, and abilities with the Access application, but it will provide you with transferable skills for working with databases in general. Lessons are designed to guide you through the essentials and then introduce you to some advanced concepts that are relevant to the workforce.

Access 2013

Section 1   Database Essentials

Unlike other Microsoft applications like Excel, Word, and PowerPoint that open immediately after initially selecting a **blank** document, **Access** is different because the database must first be given a **file name** and given a **storage location** before it can be created. So let's get started with the Access interface and concepts.

    I.   **Open a Blank Database**

    II.   **Exploring the Ribbon**

    III. **Identifying Access GUI**

    IV. **Customizing the Quick Access Toolbar**

    V.   **Close/Exit Access**

A1.1   Opening a Blank Database

1. To open **Access,** tap or click the start screen button in the lower left corner of the screen.

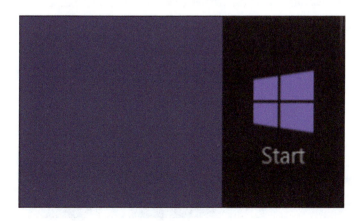

2. From the start screen begin typing *Access*. The search panel will open.

3. Select the **Blank desktop database.**

Step 3   Blank Desktop Database

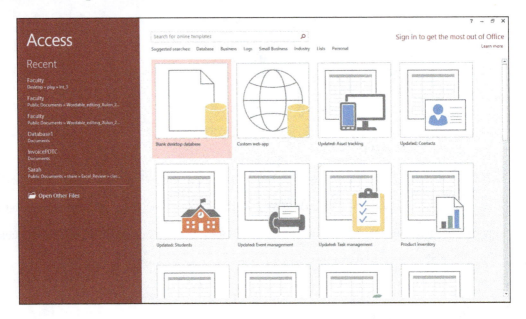

4. Select the text box field to enter a **file name** for the database. Title the database *MyUniv.*

5. Next, click the yellow folder and choose the location where you would like the database to be stored (on the computer, in the cloud, or in a storage device). Choose the Access Student Resource Folder.

6. Click **create**. (Database will be created and will open in the new location).

Step 5   Folder Location

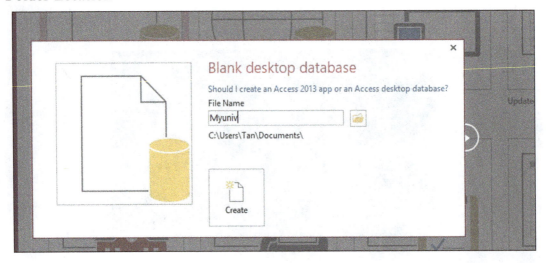

A1.2 Exploring the Ribbon

The **Ribbon** is designed with **Tab** buttons on top and **Group** associated buttons on the bottom. These commands allow you to access common tasks. Figure 1.1 shows a view of the ribbon.

Contextual Tabs are also displayed on the ribbon. However, **contextual tabs** only appear when an object is selected to give further command options for working with that particular object.

Figure 1.1   Ribbon

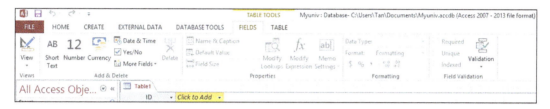

The **file** tab located on the ribbon is sometimes referred to as the **backstage view.** Printing, saving, and exporting are just a few of the many options available from this tab selection. The Ribbon can be customized to add your personal tab and group commands. To customize the tabs on the Ribbon:

1. Click **file** to access **backstage** viewing. See Figure 1.2.

Figure 1.2   File Tab

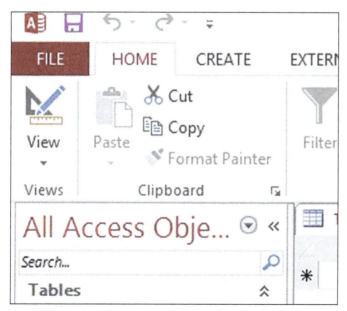

2. Select **Options** from the navigation pane on the left.

Step 2   Options

3. Click the **Customize Ribbon** command from the categories on the left. On the right, under the column, **customize the ribbon,** click **new tab** at the bottom of the dialog box.

4. Select the **new tab** and click **rename**. Enter a name for the new tab in the dialog box that appears as shown in Figure 1.3.

❖ **Note:** the new tab and new group appear together, as a set.

5. Next, select **new group** and click the **rename** tab to give the new group a name of your choice. (A **rename** dialog box will open with an *option* to choose an image).

6. With your new group selected, choose your group-associated commands. (These are the commands that you use regularly such as the font, font size, the format painter, paste. . . .)

7. Select your commands from the choices on the left and **add** them to your new group on the right.

8. Click **OK** when finished.

Figure 1.3   Customize Ribbon

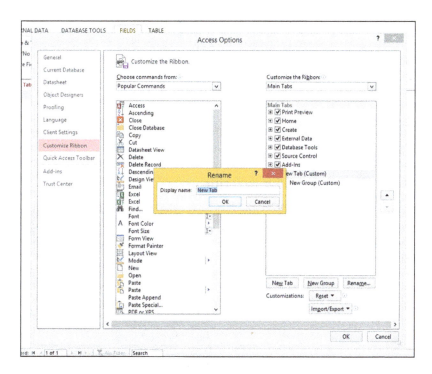

A1.3   Identifying the Access Graphical User Interface-(GUI)

Access is a collection of tables and objects that is called a **database**. The relationships between the table objects are designed to be relational. View the **Access** screen and identify the basic features.

Compare and contrast the screen in Figure 1.4 with your screen.

Refer to Table 1.1 for a Description of Access Features.

Figure 1.4   Identify the Access GUI

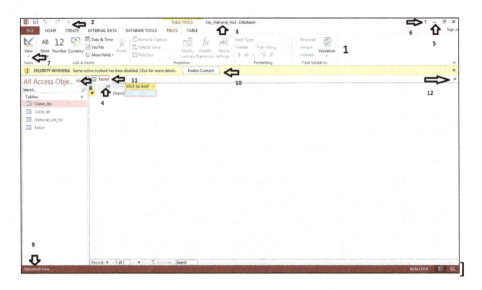

Table 1.1   GUI Word Features and Descriptions

	Features	Description
1	Ribbon	Tabs are on top. Groups are on the bottom and commands are in the middle.
2	Quick Access Toolbar	Common tasks button
3	Title Bar	Shows name of document and application name
4	Primary Key field	Unique record identifier
5	Access sizing buttons	Minimize and restore database
6	Access Help Feature	Search Access for keywords
7	Window Views	Shows Access Table Datasheet View and Design View
8	Navigation Pane	Shows all of the Access objects; Access working window pane. (Located on the left)
9	Status bar	Displays Database Information. Right click the status bar to customize.
10	Security Feature	Improved feature prompts the user to enable only trusted content
11	Table 1	Shows the default name of the object
12	Close Table	Closes the table (object).

The **Help** feature displays information about Access. Click the question, **[?]** mark that is located in the top right corner of the screen. Enter a word or phrase to search and a list of topics will be displayed. You may also access help by pressing **F1** on your keyboard.

A1.4   Customizing the Quick Access Toolbar

The **Quick Access Toolbar** allows you to add commands that are accessed regularly. The Quick Access Toolbar is located either above or below the ribbon.

1. Click the drop-down arrow to the right of the **Quick Access Toolbar** (depending on the location).
2. Select the commands that you wish to have quick access to on the toolbar, as shown in Figure 1.5.

Note: In order to choose more commands, click the **more commands** option.

Step 1   Quick Access Toolbar

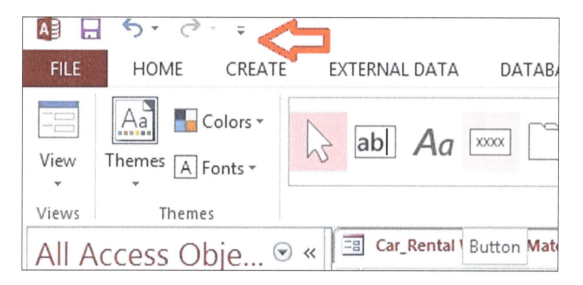

Figure 1.5   Access Options

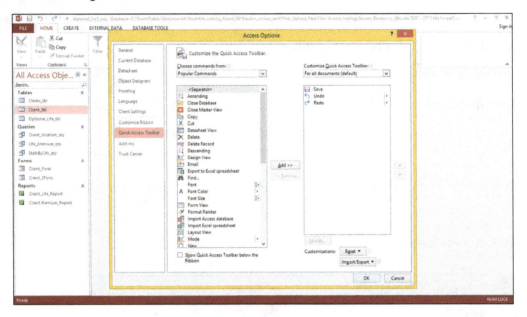

A1.5   Closing and Exiting Access

To close the database, click the **X** in the top right corner of the database. You may also:

1. Click the **file** tab.

2. Select the **close** tab from the navigation pane on the left.

3. Click **close**. (The database will close).

Step 3 Closing Access

Section 2   Defining Database Concepts and Table Structure

Student Resource Folder—(Access_2)

Before a database can be created, there are some basic steps that must be considered, such as planning the database and determining the purpose for the database. You must also determine the types of related tables needed, how to effectively relate these tables through a common field, and choose a primary key connector.

    I.   **Defining the Database Elements**

    II.   **Creating a Table in Datasheet View**

    III.   **Saving the Table**

    IV.   **Navigating in Datasheet View**

    V.   **Moving Columns**

    VI.   **Sort/Filter Records**

    VII. **Preview/Print Table**

    VIII. **Setting Margins**

    IX.   **Compact a Database**

    X.   **Backup a Database**

A2.1 Defining the Database Elements

In order to maintain and organize a database, creating tables with relationships, we must first build a foundation with some key terms and concepts.

A **field** is a single piece of information about a person, place, object, or item that is organized into categories. Figure 2.1 shows three fields: Student ID, Student Last Name, and Student First Name (fields are vertical).

The collection of fields related to one group of information is known as a **record**. Records are horizontal, such as the student record for **M73008** that is Jazmine Lebron.

A collection or group of related records make up the **table**. The table below is called the Student Information Table.

Figure 2.1   Table Fields

Student ID	Student Last Nan	Student First Nar
M73008	Lebron	Jazmine
M73025	Lady	Bryan
M73049	Allen	Kalvin
M73054	Carter	William
M73083	Bahaar	Adrianna
M73089	Chandler	Mariah
M73093	Williams	Lori
M73117	Mazyck	Trayvon
M73125	Simmons	Ana
M73138	Biran	Trevon

Table Relationship

A collection or group of related tables is called a **database.** The relationship created between these related tables makes it a **relational database**. In order to have a relationship between tables, there must be at least two tables, and the tables must have a **common field** that appears in both tables. The tables are connected through a common field. See Figures 2A and 2B.

Figure 2A   Common Field

SchoolCode	SID#	StudenLastName	StudenFirstName
100-A	M73176	Brandon	David
105-A	M73557	Marlo	Terrell
175-A	M73923	Robinson	Malry
176-A	M73089	Chandler	Mariah
227-A	M73742	Harris	Zachery
237-A	M73258	Hubbard	Wade
240-A	M73049	Allen	Kalvin
288-A	M73083	Bahaar	Adrianna
310-A	M73008	Lebron	Jazmine
310-B	M73054	Carter	William

School_Information

Foreign Key

Common Field

Primary Key

Figure 2B   Primary Key

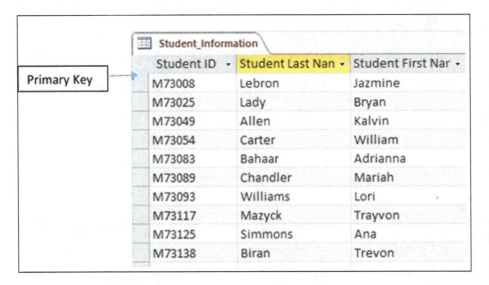

Primary Key

In order to create a database that will operate effectively, a primary key is required. A **primary key** is a field that uniquely identifies each record in a table. The primary key field **cannot** be duplicated, nor can a primary key field be empty or **null**. In other words, no two records should have the same identical primary key value. In Figures 2A and 2B, each student can be uniquely identified by their Student ID. No two students have the same Student ID.

Foreign Key

When the primary key field from the first table is included in the second table, this is known as the **foreign key**.

Planning

When preparing to create a database, **planning** is the first step in this process and important decisions must be made concerning the structure of the database. (For example, the School of the Arts would like you to track the students that attend their schools across the country.) Determine the following:

- What is it that you want to track?
- What do you want to answer or be able to query?
- What fields will you need to include?

- What are the names of the fields? See Table 2.1 for Field Naming Conventions.

- What are the sizes needed for each field?

- What are the data types needed for each field?

Data Types

Determining how the data will be entered into a field is a very important part of planning. Each field must be assigned a data type either manually or automatically through Access or the database designer. The **data type** determines the type of information or value that can be entered into the field and the other properties that will be attached to the field. There are many data types to choose from; see Table 2.2 for data types.

Table 2.1   Field Naming Conventions

Field Names Guidelines

- Can be up to 64 characters long
- Can include any combination of letters, numbers, spaces and special characters except a period (.), an exclamation point (!), an accent grave ('), and brackets [ ].
- Can't begin with leading spaces
- Can't include control characters (ASCII values 0 through 31)
- Can't include a double quotation mark (") in table view, or stored procedure names in a Microsoft Access project.

Table 2.2   Data Types

Data Type	Description	Field Size
Short Text	Alpha-numeric data	Up to 255 characters
Long Text	(formerly "Memo" Large amounts of alpha-numeric data	Up to about 1 GB (controls for display are limited to 64,000 characters
Number	Numeric data	1, 2, 4, 8 or 16 bytes
Date/Time	Dates and times	8 bytes
Currency	Monetary data stored with 4 decimal places of precision	8 bytes
Auto Number	Unique assigned by Access for each new record	4 bytes (16 bytes ReplicationID
Yes/No	Boolean (true/false) data: Access stores numeric value zero (0) for false, and (-1) for true	1 byte
Ole Object	Pictures, graphs or other Active X from another Windows based application	Up to 2 GB
Hyperlink	A link address to a file or document on the internet, intranet on a local area network (LAN), or your local computer	Up to 8,192 (each part of a hyperlink data type can contain up to 2048 characters).
Attachment	Files with pictures or documents; attachment field can contain an unlimited number of attachments per record, up to the storage limit of the size of a database file.	Up to 2 GB
Calculated	An expression created that uses data from one or more fields. Different result data types can be designated from the expression.	This data type is dependent on the result type property data type. Short text data type can have up to 243 characters. Long text, number, yes/no and date/time should match their respective data types.
Lookup Wizard	Not really a data type. Wizard assist with setting up the lookup field.	This field is dependent on the data type of the lookup field.

A2.2   Creating a Table in Datasheet View

Datasheet view displays data in a spreadsheet format. Columns and rows are displayed much like the grid in Excel. Searching for records is easy with the navigation bar in datasheet view.

1. Open the **MyUniv** Database.
2. The database opens with **Table 1** included by default, as shown in Figure 2.3. (**Note**: the table has not been saved at this point). By default, Access makes the primary key field **ID** as the first field in the table and the default data type is **auto number.**

3. Right click the **ID** field name and select rename to rename the field, type *SID#* for Student Identification Number.

4. Click the tab to move to the next field; notice that the drop-down tab will appear for you to select the data type.

5. Select **short text** and notice the field name is now selected; type [**StudentLastName**].

6. The completed table has four fields, as shown in Figure 2.4. Repeat steps 4 and 5 to add the additional fields to the table.

7. See Table 2–3 for **field** names and **data types**.

8. **Continue** to save table.

Figure 2.3   Access Table 1

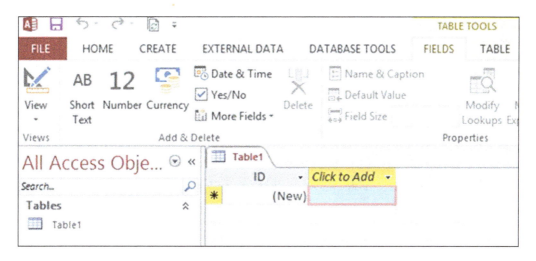

Table 2.3   Data Types

Field Name	Data Type
SID#	Short text
StudentLastName	Short text
StudentFirstName	Short text
School#	Short text

Figure 2.4   Table Field Results

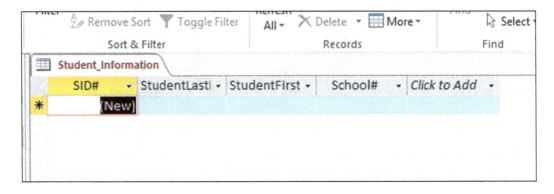

A2.3   Saving the Table

There are a few ways to save the table. Once the table has been initially saved and given a name, it will automatically save the information that is entered.

1. Click the **file** tab.
2. Select **save.** A dialog box appears, as shown in Figure 2.5.
3. Type in the field, [**Student_Information**].
4. Click **OK.**
5. The table is now saved. The table name appears in the navigation pane on the left and on the tab at the top of the table. See Figure 2.6.

Figure 2.5   Saving a Database Table

Figure 2.6   Saved Table

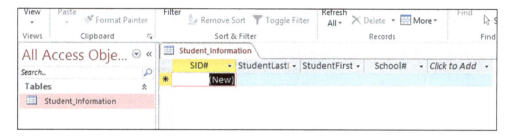

Changing the Data Type for the Automatically Generated Primary Key Field

6. Now let's reopen the table in Datasheet view.

7. Double click the **Student_Information** table to open it. Select the **Primary Key** field **SID#.** (Notice that the **Table Tools** contextual tab opens).

8. Click on the **Fields** tab; click the down arrow for the **Data Type** command in the **Formatting** group.

9. Select **short text**.

10. **Continue** to add records.

A2.4   Navigating in Datasheet View

The record indicator displays the records in the table. See Figure 2.7. The arrow indicators show first record, next record, last record and also opens a new blank record.

Figure 2.7   Record Indicator

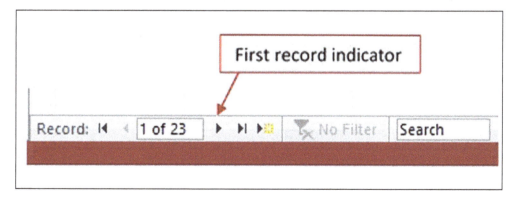

Database Objects

The objects of a database help to maintain, collect, and display information. Table 2.4 shows the Access database objects.

Table 2.4   Objects of a Database

Object	Description
Table	Organized records that are made up by columns and rows.
Query	Most common feature is to retrieve specific data from tables. However, used to perform calculations.
Form	An interface other than a datasheet view used to enter, edit and view records.
Report	The presentation of data in tables or queries.
Macro	Automating repetitive tasks.
Module	Automated actions similar to macros, but through programming using Visual Basic Applications

A2.4.1   Opening a Table from the Navigation Pane

Double click the table from the **navigation** pane on the left to open the table.

Closing a Table

Close the table by clicking the **X** to the far right of the table name. (**Note:** be careful not to close the database). 8.

Adding Records

1. With the **MyUniv** database open,
2. Double click the table **Student_Information**.
3. Enter the information found in Table 2.5. Tab to move to the next field after you enter the information in each field.
4. Continue until all records are entered.

Table 2.5   Student Information

Student_Information			
SID#	StudenLastName	StudenFirstName	School#
M73008	Lebron	Jazmine	310
M73025	Lady	Bryan	715
M73049	Allen	Kalvin	240
M73054	Carter	William	310
M73083	Bahaar	Adrianna	288
M73089	Chandler	Mariah	176
M73093	Williams	Lori	747
M73117	Mazyck	Trayvon	806

Deleting Records

Once a record has been deleted, that primary key value can no longer be used. Therefore, use caution when deleting records. Access will always prompt you before a record is deleted as a safety precaution.

1. Move the mouse pointer to the left of the first field for record **M73008**. After the mouse turns into a **black arrow** pointing toward the right, select the record. (Selected records will be highlighted).
2. From the **Home** tab in the **Records** group, click the **Delete** command.
3. Click **yes**.
4. The record indicator will show seven records remaining.
5. Click **save** and **continue**.

Step 3 Delete Records

A2.5 Moving Columns

Your table can be modified or rearranged by moving columns from one place in the table to another.

1. With the **Student_Information** table still open,

2. Select the column **School#** to move. Hover your mouse over the field header until the mouse changes to a four-headed arrow.

3. Click and drag to move to the second column.

4. Release mouse. Column will show in new position, as shown in Figure 2.8.

Figure 2.8   Moving Columns

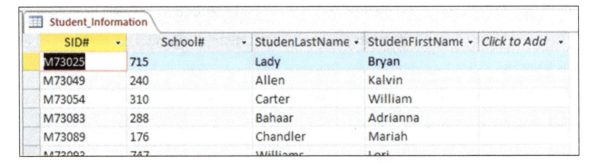

Hiding Fields (Columns)

In order to hide columns in a table that you do not wish to display or print:

1. Right click the column, SID#.

2. Select **hide fields** from the sub-menu that pops up.

3. The column will disappear.

To Unhide Fields (Columns)

1. Right click a column.

2. Select the column that you wish to **Unhide** (SID#) as shown in Figure *2.9*

3. Click **close** when finished.

4. **Close the Student_information** table.

Figure 2.9   Unhide Columns

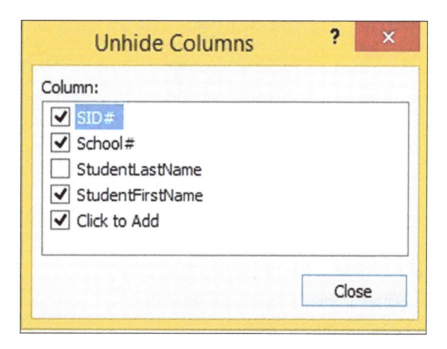

A2.6   Sort/Filter Records

Sorting records help to organize your data and filtering allows you to hide data that you do not want to display.

There are many ways to sort data, depending on the information stored in the field. Sorting can be done by dates, names, state, or other ways. Sorts can be arranged in chronological order or reverse order.

1. Open the **Arts** database.

2. Open the **School_Information** table.

3. Select the field, [**StudentLastName**] to sort.

4. From the **Home** tab in the **Sort & Filter** group.

5. Select the **Ascending** command.

6. Records will reflect the change, as shown in Figure 2.10.

7. **Continue**.

Figure 2.10   Record Results

SID#	School#	StudentLastName	StudenFirstName	Enrollment Date
M73049	240	Allen	Kalvin	08/28/2006
M73083	288	Bahaar	Adrianna	01/07/2006
M73054	310	Carter	William	08/28/2006
M73089	176	Chandler	Mariah	08/28/2006
M73025	715	Lady	Bryan	08/28/2006
M73117	806	Mazyck	Trayvon	09/19/2006
M73093	747	Williams	Lori	08/28/2006

Filtering

Filtering allows you to display only the data that you want to see in the table.

1. Select the drop-down arrow next to the field to be filtered.

2. Select the field [**School#**]. **Select All** and then deselect **All.**

3. Check the box for **240** and **288** from the list.

4. The table has filtered all records **except** records 240 and 288 of the School# field.

5. From the **Home** tab, click the **Toggle** command in the **Sort & Filter** group to remove the filter. (**Note** filters are only temporary).

Filter by Selection

Filter by selection allows you to select specific data from your table. This filter is very convenient, especially when you are searching through lots of data and you want to search for specific words or phrases that contain parts of another word. (Example: all words with strawberry included in it).

1. Click in the cell **Duke Performing Arts**.

2. From the **Home** tab, select the down-pointing arrow for the **Selection** command in the **Sort & Filter** group.

3. Select, **Equals Duke Performing Arts**. (**Note**: only those records that have Duke Performing Arts appear, as shown in Figure 2.11).

4. To remove filter, click the **Toggle Filter** command in the **Sort & Filter** group.

Figure 2.11   Filter By Selections

A2.7   Preview/Print Table

Previewing before printing saves time and money. Access gives you the option to not only print reports, but printing can be done from any of the Access objects. Tables and queries can be printed to show only the fields that need to appear while protecting confidential record information.

1. With the **School_Information** table still open,

2. Click the **file** tab and select **print.**

3. Click **print preview** to review the document before printing. Print document when ready.

4. Click the **X** to close the **Print Preview** tab.

5. **Continue**.

Step 3   Print Command

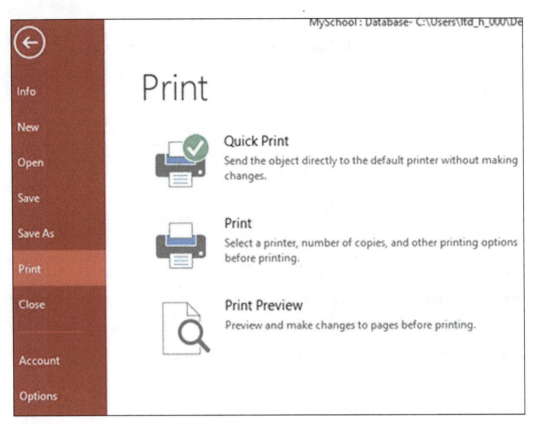

A2.8   Setting Margins

Once a document has been previewed, there may be a need to make adjustments to the margins.

Review the **Print Preview** tab (as shown in Figure 2.12) to make changes to the document's **page size** and **page layout**.

Figure 2.12   Print Preview Tab

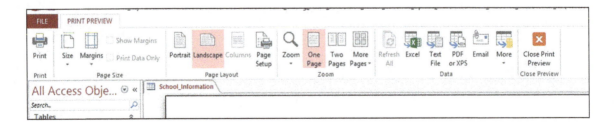

A2.9 Compact a Database

The size of a database expands very quickly from entering and deleting records, and so forth. When things are deleted or replaced, the space that it once occupied is not automatically replaced by the incoming or replaced data. Because of this process, Access has built into the database a system to **compact** and **repair** the database.

Compacting the database is a system that rearranges the data and the objects in the database to decrease its file size, which in effect gives you more disk space. This process helps to improve the speed of opening and closing the database. Access performs the repair as it compacts the database.

1. Open the database file that you want to **compact** and **repair**. Select the **Arts** database.
2. Select the **file** tab.
3. Next, select the **Compact & Repair** command.
4. If Access repairs the database or corrupted files, it will display a message.

Step 3   Compact & Repair

A2.10 Backup a Database

Backing up a database is a process that should be done regularly. Making a copy of the database protects your information from loss or damage. Keeping track of the backup date information will help you to restore files with the latest recapture date.

Access has a system in place to help you keep up with the backup process. Access will create a default filename for your backup copy that consists of keeping the original filename as the file that is being backed up plus the current date of the database backup. (For example, MyUniv plus the current date). Follow the steps below to back up your database.

1. Open the database needing to be backed up. (Open MyUniv.)
2. Click the **file** tab.
3. Select **save as** and select **Back Up Database**.

Step 3   Back Up Database

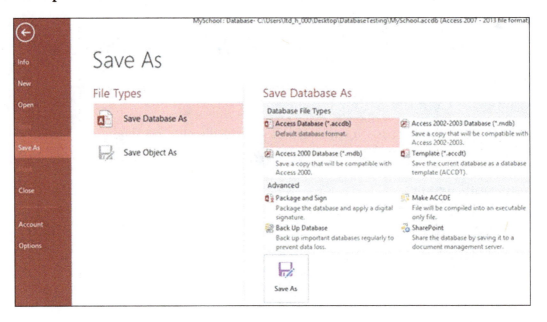

Section 3 Working with Tables and Relationships

While tables can be created in Datasheet view, the field property adjustments and table structure are completed in Design view. Creating relationships between tables is why Access is referred to as a **relational database.**

I. **Creating a Table in Design View**

II. **Modify Field Properties**

III. **Creating Input Masks**

IV. **Create a Lookup Column**

V. **Create a Validation Rule**

VI. **Moving and Deleting Fields in Design View**

VII. **Creating Relationships**

VIII. **Define Subdatasheet View**

A3.1 Creating a Table in Design View

We have previously created a table in datasheet view; however, there is another way to create a table in Access that will allow you to design the table structure first and enter the data later. This is called **design view.** (**Note**: To create additional tables click: Create>Table)

1. Open a **blank desktop database**.

2. Name the database **MyNFL** and place it in the Access Resource Folder.

3. Switch to **design view** to create the table, but first save the table as **Season2014_2015**.

4. Click the down arrow for the **View** command in the **Views** group to switch to **Design View**. (Design view opens in a grid with the **Primary Key** field and symbol selected, as shown in Figure 3.1).

5. Select the primary key field and rename it **TeamID**. Keep the default data type of autonumber.

6. Select the next row and enter the remaining field information, as shown in Table 3.1. (See the completed table in Figure 3.2).

7. **Continue**.

Figure 3.1   Primary Key Indicator

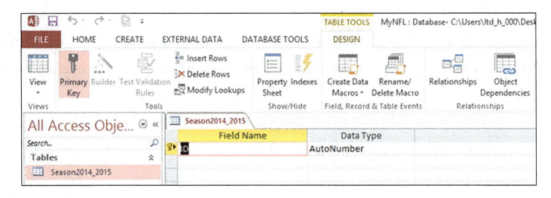

Table 3.1   Design View Table Data

Field Name	Data Type
Team_Name	Short Text
Conference	Short Text
Division	Short Text
City	Short Text
State	Short Text
Wins	Number
Loses	Number
Super_Bowl	Yes/No

Figure 3.2   Table Completed

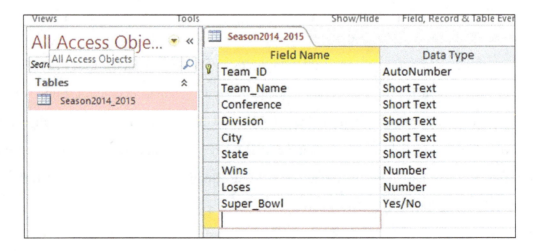

A3.2   Modifying Fields and Field Properties

In design view, the bottom grid or **field properties** is where you control the different field settings. Setting a field size controls how much information the user can enter into a field. The **field properties** grid provides the structure for the database and controls and maintains the data field entries.

Changing the Field Size

Changing the **field size** not only preserves the size of the database, but it will also establish a pattern for consistency. In this example we will change the **State** field size.

1. With the **Season2014_2015** table open, in datasheet view,
2. Select the **design view** command in the **views** group.
3. Select the **state** field (from the top grid) and select the **General** tab from the **field properties** grid, as shown in Figure 3.3.
4. Click in the **field size** and change it to [2].
5. **Continue**.

Note: If a field property is changed after records have been entered, Access will display several warning messages notifying you that, some data may be lost. An example of this would be if you changed the field size of a field that has records entered in it from the default field size of 255 to a smaller number, Access will truncate the data.

Figure 3.3   Field Properties

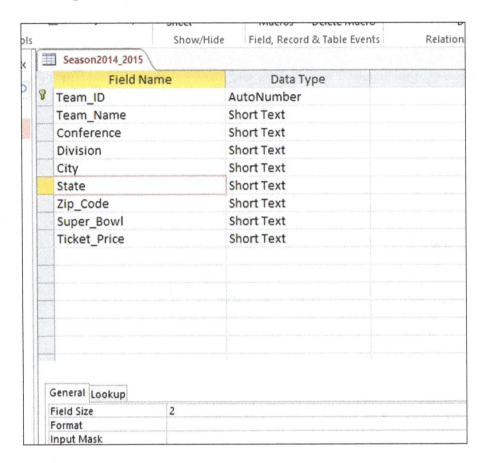

A3.2.1   Adding Fields to a Table in Design View

1. With the **Season2014_2015** table still open.

2. Place the insertion point in the row following **Super_Bowl**.

3. Type [**Zip_Code**].

4. Add another field in the next row and type [**Ticket_Price**].

5. Data types for both new fields are **short text,** as shown in Figure 3.4.

6. **Continue**.

Figure 3.4   Data Types

Field Name	Data Type
Team_ID	AutoNumber
Team_Name	Short Text
Conference	Short Text
Division	Short Text
City	Short Text
State	Short Text
Wins	Number
Loses	Number
Super_Bowl	Yes/No
Zip_Code	Short Text
Ticket_Price	Short Text

(Table title tab: Season2014_2015)

A3.3   Creating an Input Mask

An **Input mask** displays data in a specific pattern, which helps make data easier to read. An input mask can be placed on social security numbers, phone numbers, zip codes, and more. A placeholder is inserted for the user's input and to control data entry. See Table 3.2 for a description of Input Mask Codes. For this exercise, we will place an **input mask** on the **zip_code** field.

1. With the **Season2014_2015** table still open in design view,
2. Select the **zip_code** field.
3. Click the three dots to the right of the **input mask,** in the **field properties** grid. **(Click yes, if prompted to save).**
4. An **input mask** dialog box appears, as shown in Figure 3.5.
5. Select the **zip code** input mask.
6. Click **next** and choose the # symbol placeholder for the zip code field entry.
7. Click in the **try it** field and enter a 9 digit zip code for testing purposes.
8. Click **next**, then choose the **1st** button (**with the symbols**).
9. Click **next.**

10. Click **finish**. (Notice the input mask code in the field properties).

Step 3 Input Mask Field Properties

Figure 3.5 Input Mask Wizard

Table 3.2   **Input Mask Codes Description**

Input Mask Character	Description
0	User must enter a digit 0-9
9	User can enter a digit 0-9
#	User can enter a digit, space, plus or minus sign
L	User must enter a letter
?	User can enter a letter
A	User must enter a letter or a digit
a	User can enter a letter or a digit
&	User must enter a character or a space
C	User can enter characters or spaces
.,;; - /	Decimal and thousands placeholder, date and time separators. The character selected is dependent upon the Windows regional settings
>	Converts all characters following to upper case
<	Converts all characters following to lower case
!	Causes the input mask to fill from left to right instead, from right to left
\	Characters immediately following will be displayed literally.
""	Characters displayed in quotations will be displayed literally.

Note: The input mask code is made up of one mandatory part and two optional parts with each part separated by a semicolon.

A3.3.1   Add a Record and Test the Input Mask

1. Click the **view** tab in the **views** group to return to **datasheet view**.

2. Click **yes** when prompted to save table.

3. Enter a record for your favorite NFL team. Pay close attention to the **zip_code** field with the placeholder inserted.

4. **Continue**.

Step 3   New Record Entry

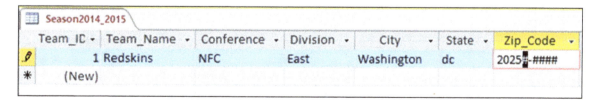

A3.4   Creating a Lookup Column

A **lookup column** (field) restricts the data that is entered into a field. This limits the user to a specific set of choices. Working with a lookup column can make a big difference when creating queries.

1.   Switch to the design view of the **Season2014_2015** table.
2.   We will change the check boxes for the super_bowl field to a pull-down field with a list of choices to select from.
3.   Pull the arrow down in the data type of the super_bowl field and select **lookup wizard**. (A **Lookup Wizard** dialog box will appear).
4.   Choose the second radio button (**I will type in the values that I want**).
5.   Click **next.**

Step 4   Lookup Wizard

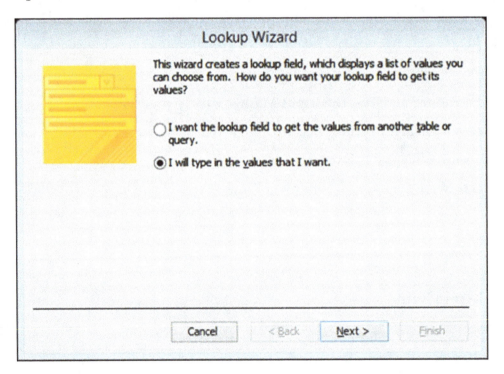

6.   Set the number of columns to [1] and type *Yes* in the first column and *No* in the second column, as shown in Figure 3.6.
7.   Click **next**.
8.   Click **finish**. (**Note**: the **super_bowl** field data type is now short text).

9. Switch back to datasheet view.

10. Select the record you previously entered and pull the arrow down in the **super_bowl** field and make a selection from the list, as shown in Figure 3.7.

11. Switch back to design view.

12. **Continue**.

Figure 3.6   Lookup Column

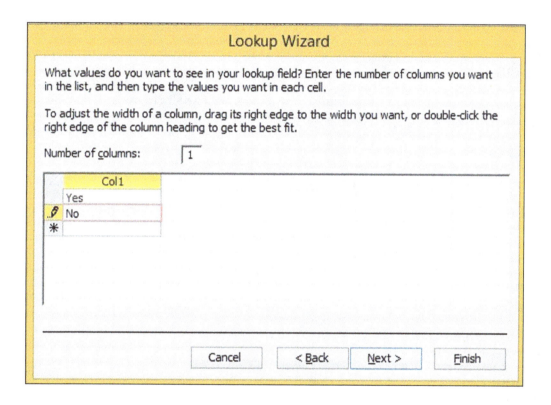

Figure 3.7   Lookup Field Selection

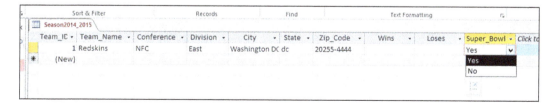

A3.5   Creating a Validation Rule

Validation Rules are created to prevent user data entry errors. Validation Rules can be used to enter a statement for the user when the data entry for a field does not meet the criteria.

1. With the **Season2014_2015** table still open in design view,

2. Select the **Ticket_Price** field.

3. Make sure the **General** tab in the Field Properties is selected.

4. Select the **Validation Rule** in the field properties and type *< 500*.

5. Select the **Validation Text** in the field properties and type *Please enter a value less than 500.*

6. Switch back to datasheet view and test the record previously entered.

7. Click in the field for the **Ticket_Price** and try entering an amount greater than 500.

8. When you enter an amount exceeding the validation rule, Access will give you a warning, as shown in Figure 3.8.

9. Click **OK**.

10. Now reenter a value less than five hundred, and the warning will disappear.

11. Switch back to **design view**.

12. **Continue**.

Step 4   Validation Rule

General Lookup	
Field Size	255
Format	
Input Mask	
Caption	
Default Value	
Validation Rule	< 500
Validation Text	Please enter a value less than 500.
Required	No

Figure 3.8   Validation Text

A3.6   Moving and Deleting Fields in Design View

Moving Fields in Design View

1. Position the mouse to the left of the **zip_code** field to select it.

2. Click, hold and drag to the new position. (**Notice**: a white rectangle appears at the bottom of the arrow.)

3. Move the **zip_code** field after the state field, then release the mouse.

4. **Continue**.

Step 2   Moving Fields in Design View

Field Name	Data Type
Team_ID	AutoNumber
Team_Name	Short Text
Conference	Short Text
Division	Short Text
City	Short Text
State	Short Text
Zip_Code	Short Text
Wins	Number
Loses	Number
Super_Bowl	Yes/No
Ticket_Price	Short Text

A3.6.1   Deleting Fields in Design View

1. Select the **wins** field. Notice the **Table Tools** contextual tab appears.

2. On the **Design** tab of the **Tools** group, select the **delete rows** command. (Click **yes,** if asked to permanently delete field.)

3. Repeat step 3 to delete the **losses** field.

4. Switch to **datasheet view** to verify the changes.

5. **Close** the table.

Step 1   Deleting Fields in Design View

Season2014_2015	
Field Name	Data Type
Team_ID	AutoNumber
Team_Name	Short Text
Conference	Short Text
Division	Short Text
City	Short Text
State	Short Text
Zip_Code	Short Text
Wins	Number
Loses	Number
Super_Bowl	Short Text

Step 2   Deleting Rows in Design View

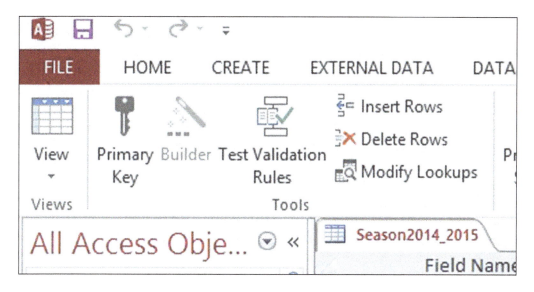

A3.7   Creating Relationships

The purpose of a relational database is to eliminate redundancy (duplicate data), and Access was designed to be a relational database. Relationships exist between two or more tables through a common field join. Access has three types of relationships, one-to-one, one-to-many, and many-to-many. The most common being one-to-many.

In a relationship between tables, one table must be the primary table and the other table is considered the related table. In a **one-to-many** relationship, the table that is referred to as the **one** is considered as the **primary** table, and the table that is referred to as the **many** is known as the **related** table.

The **symbol** for a one-to-many relationship is a **[1]** for the primary table and an **[infinity]** symbol for the related table, as shown in Figure 3.8.

Access determines the type of relationship based on the common field that joins the two tables together. The process of relating tables together is called a **join**. In a one-to-many relationship, at least one record must exist in the primary table, while there may be zero or many records existing in the related table. In the example below, a client can only have one claim# in the primary table with zero to many rental claims under the same claim# in the related table.

Figure 3.8   Relationship Symbols

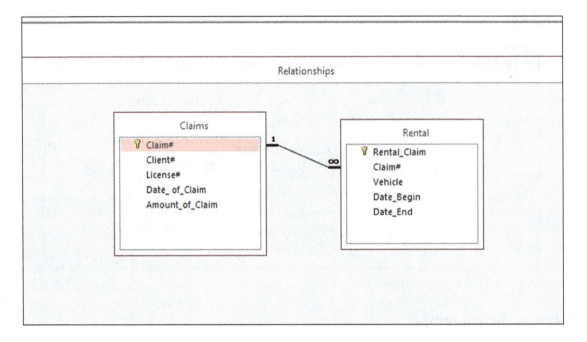

Referential Integrity

In order to create a proper working relational database, there must be rules to adhere to. The rules that govern and enforce the consistency of the database is called **referential integrity.** Whenever you create a relationship between related tables, you have the option of enforcing rules of integrity. Once these rules are chosen, Access will enforce all rules that govern the database.

Records that are entered into the related table and not entered into the primary table creates **orphan records** with inconsistent data, and Access will not create a relationship without some adjustments being made.

Cascade update is used so that records can be updated across all related fields in the related tables. Should you decide to add the orphan record to the primary table, Access will permit the change as long as there is no duplication of the primary key or matching records in the related table. Consequently, choosing the cascade update option would eliminate the possibility of having inconsistent data, and Access would update all related fields and accept the change.

Cascade delete will delete all records in both the primary table as well as the related table. Otherwise, if you choose to delete records in the primary table and there are matching records that exist in the related table, Access will not allow the deletion.

Note: Use caution when applying the cascade delete because while there are advantages to this option, there are also some disadvantages. Deleting records inadvertently is irreversible.

Creating a One-to-Many Relationship

1. Open the **National_Ins3** database.
2. Click the **Database Tools** tab.
3. Select the **Relationships** command in the **Relationships** group, as shown in Figure 3.9.
4. If the tables are not showing in the Relationship window, select the **show table** command in the **relationships** group, as shown in Figure 3.10.

Figure 3.9   Creating Relationships

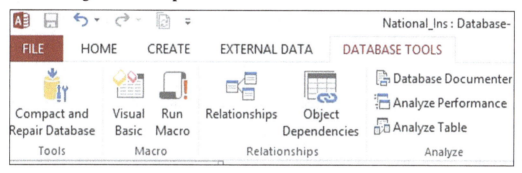

Figure 3.10   Show Table

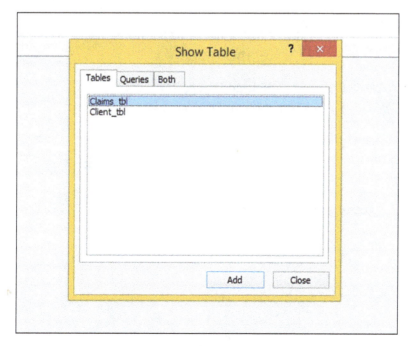

5. Select the **Tables** tab and **add** the Client_tbl and the Claims_tbl. Close the **show table** dialog box.

6. Create a **one-to-many relationship** between the Client_tbl and the Claims_tbl with the common field **Client_Policy#,** as shown in Figure 3.11.

7. Select the client_policy# from the Client_tbl, hold and drag (the mouse will have a rectangle attached to it with a black cross inside) the pointer to the Client_Policy# in the claims_tbl and then release the mouse.

8. An **Edit Relationships** dialog box will appear showing the two fields, one from the primary table and the other from the related table.

   ❖ Notice the Cascade Update and Cascade Delete boxes are grayed out; they will not become available unless the Enforce Referential Integrity box is checked.

   ❖ Should you choose not to check the Enforce Referential Integrity box, you will only have a common field join, and Access cannot enforce the integrity of the database.

9. Check the **Enforce Referential Integrity** box, this will create the one-to-many relationship type that Access shows is possible at the bottom of the dialog box.

10. Click **create**. Notice that the one-to-many relationship is created.

11. **Close** the **Relationship Tools** window.

Step 8   Enforce Referential Integrity

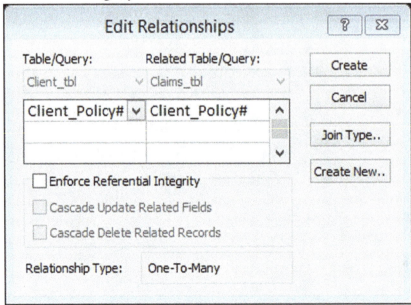

Figure 3.11   Client Policy Relationship Established

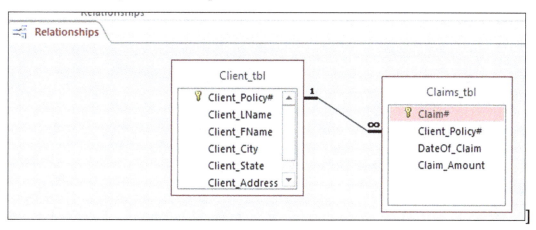

❖ **Note:** When creating relationships, the common field that joins the two tables must have the same data type, or Access will give you an error message, as shown in Figure 3.12. And the two tables will not be joined.

Figure 3.12   Incorrect Data Type Error

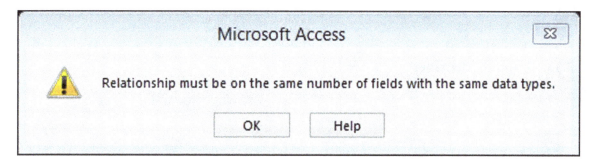

Creating a One-to-One Relationship

In a **one-to-one** relationship both the primary table and the related table contain only one record through a common field that has matching data. For this example, we will create a one-to-one relationship by first establishing a one-to-many relationship and then by changing the index for the key fields in both tables. Note: both the common field (usually the primary key and foreign key fields) must have a unique index. In this example a client can opt out of purchasing the optional life policy.

1. With the **National_Ins3** database open.
2. Open the Optional_Life_tbl in datasheet view.

3. Select the **Fields** tab from the **Table Tools** contextual tab and select the **Short Text** command from the **Add & Delete** group.

4. With the field selected, click the **More Fields** down arrow and select **Lookup & Relationship.** (a lookup dialog box will open).

5. Choose next because you want to look up values from another table. Select the Client_tbl and select next.

6. From the **Available Fields** choose the Client_Policy# field and move it to the **Selected Fields**

7. Click **next** (three times).

8. Name the field Client_Policy#. **Note**: (enforcing referential integrity is not required for this example).

9. Click **Finish**. **Note**: (your Client_Policy# field now includes a drop down and it is a foreign key).

10. Now select the Client_Policy# field. Select **fields** from the **Table Tools** contextual tab and check the **indexed** and **unique** box. See Figure 3.13

    Note: The relationship window shows the established one-to-one relationship without the symbols, as shown in Figure 3.14. Design view of the table also shows the indexed property for the Client_Policy# field. **Note** only two of the three values can be used in a one-to-one relationship, (No, or Yes(No Duplicates).

Figure 3.13   Unique Identifier

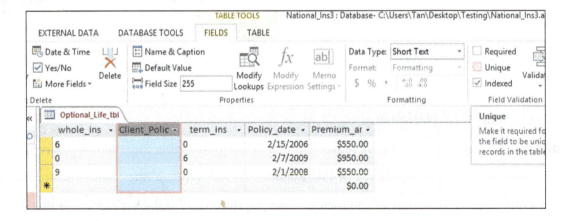

Figure 3.14   One-to-One Relationship

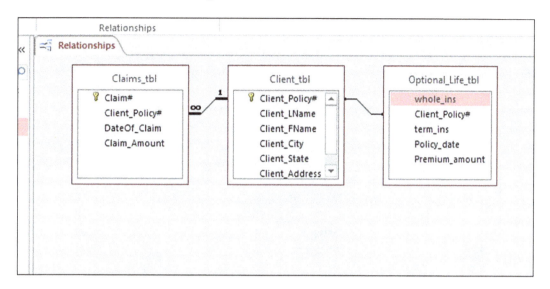

11. Next, open the Optional_Life_tbl in data sheet view and select (P1585, P1625 and P7725) for the 3 records of the Client_Policy# field.

    [**Hint** – common fields do not have to have the same field name, but the field data type (values) must be the same]

A3.8   Viewing Records in Subdatasheet View

After two related tables are joined, you are able to view the related records from the primary table by displaying the subdatasheet. Click the plus sign or expand indicator that appears next to the record for viewing.

1. With the **National_Ins3** database still open,

2. Open the **Client_tbl** in datasheet view.

3. Click on the **plus sign** to view the record in the related table, as shown in Figure 3.15.

4. The **Subdatasheet** opens.

    ❖ **Note:** should the table have more than one relationship created, Access will open an Insert Subdatasheet dialog box for you to select the Subdatasheet you would like to view. See Figure 3.16.

5. **Close** the table and the database.

Note: The advantage of displaying the subdatasheet is the ability to edit a table while viewing the information from the related table.

Figure 3.15   Subdatasheet View

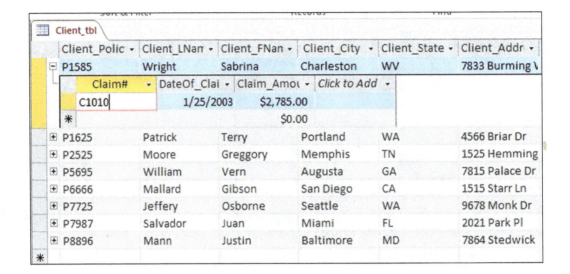

Figure 3.16   Inserting Subdatasheet Table Views

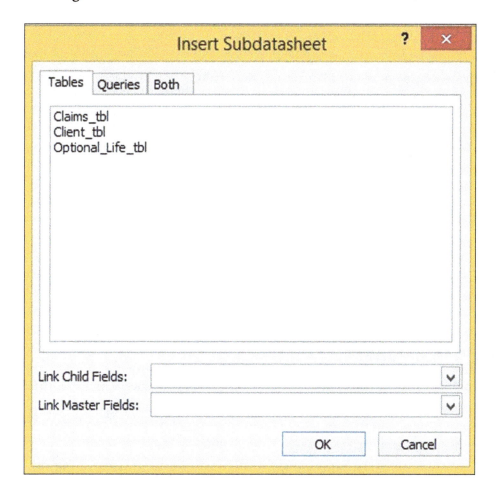

Section 4   Working with Queries and Other Database Objects

Queries are objects that allow you to view and analyze your data from a different perspective while providing meaningful answers to questions. Forms and Reports are Access objects that can be used to display database information and include control objects that perform statistical calculations or give instructions.

I.   **Creating a Select Query**

II.   **Performing Calculations in a Query**

III. **Creating a Form**

IV.   **Creating a Split Form**

V.   **Creating a Report using the Report Tool**

Section 4

A4.1   Creating a Select Query

A **query** is an object that extracts information to answer specific questions about the data stored in the database. **Example**: How many clients live in Virginia? Creating a query will help answer these types of questions to keep you from sorting through each individual record, which can be excessive if the database is huge.

A query will show only the records that you are seeking, give you answers to specific data, perform calculations, combine data from other tables, and change or delete information from other tables in your database.

Access has many types of queries to choose from; therefore, your queries should be determined based on the information needed. Queries can be created using the Query Wizard or design your own. The results of a query are referred to as a **recordset** because it displays your answers in a datasheet view of records that are specific to your questions.

Creating a Query in Design View

1. Open the **National_Ins4** database.

2. Select the **create** tab.

3. Select the **Query Design** command from the **Queries** group. A Show Table dialog box will open, as shown in Figure 4.1.

Figure 4.1   Query Design View

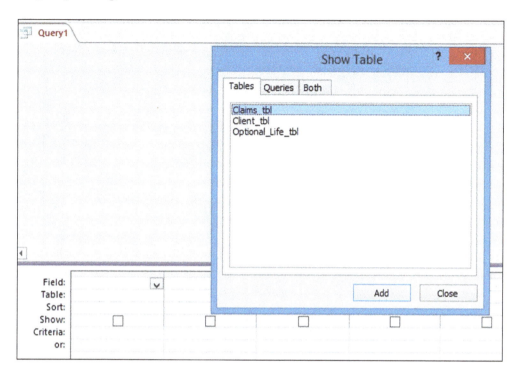

4. Select the **Tables** tab, then **add** the client_tbl to the query grid. (**Notice** the table shows all of the fields in the table).

5. **Close** the dialog box.

6. The design grid is where the fields are placed for the query. (**Hint:** a query is not a duplication of a table; so all of the fields from the table are not necessary in a query.)

7. Select the **client_policy#**, hold and drag to the first column in the query design grid, and release the mouse, as shown in Figure 4.2 or double click the field in the table and it will automatically be added to the query design grid.

8. Repeat to add the remaining fields to the query grid, **[Client_LName, Client_FName, Client_State].**

9. Click the **Run** command (to run the query results) in the **Results** group of the **Query Tools** contextual tab. See Figure 4.3. (**Note**: the query results are displayed in a recordset in datasheet view, and only a select number of fields are displayed).

10. **Close** and **save the** query by clicking the **X** for the query (not the database).

11. Title the query **Client_location_qry.**

Figure 4.2   Creating a Query in Design View

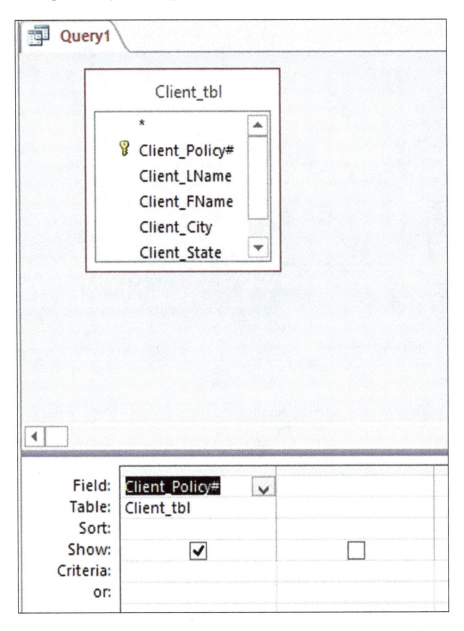

Figure 4.3   Query Results

A4.1.1   Sorting a Query in Design View

1. Right click the **Client_location_qry.** Select design view.

2. Click in the **Sort** row of the **Client_LName** field and select **Ascending,**

3. This puts the information for this query in ascending order by last name.

4. **Run** the query again to view the results.

5. **Continue**.

Step 3 Sorting a Query

A4.1.2 Adding Query Criteria

1. Open the **Client_location_qry** in design view.

2. Click in the **criteria** row of the **Client_State** field.

3. Type [*MD*].

4. **Run** the query. (You should have 3 record results).

5. **Save and Close** table.

Step 3   Query Criteria

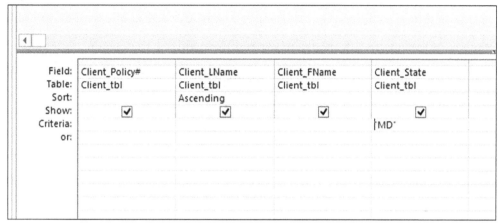

A4.2   Performing Calculations in a Query

Queries have many functions; in addition to extracting and sorting data in a database, you can use a query to perform calculations. Fields that have mathematical figures can be added or multiplied in a query. In order to give the new calculated field a **field name**, type the name of the new field followed by a colon and then the mathematical expression for the calculated value.

1. Open the **life_premium_qry** in design view.
2. Click in the blank field to the right of the premium_amount field.
3. Click the **Builder** command in the **Query Setup** group. The Expression Builder dialog box opens.

   ❖ **Click** the life_premium_qry under **Expression Elements** (If the fields of the query do not show in the next column).

4. Double click the **premium_amount** field from the **Expression Categories**. The field appears in brackets at the top of the expression dialog box.
5. Click the **operators** tab in the **Expression Elements** to view a list of the **Expressions Values**.
6. Double click the **asterisk** from the **Expression Values** to multiply, as shown in Figure 4.4.
7. Type [.*05*].
8. Click **OK** when done.

9. To expand the width of the column. Position the mouse to the right of the vertical boundary line for the calculated field until the pointer changes to a black vertical line with a left-and-right-pointing arrow, then double click the left mouse to expand the width of the column.

10. Select the title portion of the calculated field before the colon **[Expr1]** and replace it with **Premium_ Fee,** as in shown Figure 4.5.

11. **Run** the query.

12. Return to **design view**.

13. **Continue**.

Figure 4.4   Query Expression Builder

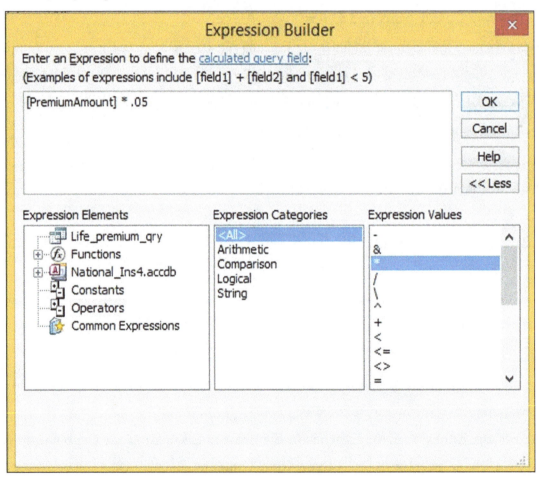

Figure 4.5   Query Calculated Field

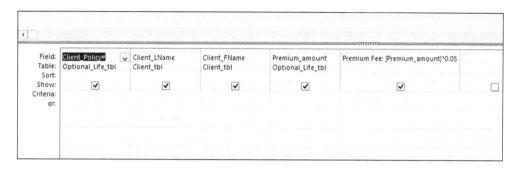

A4.2.1   Show/Hide Columns in a Query Grid

1. With the **life_premium_qry** open in design view,

2. Uncheck the **show** box in the life_policy# field.

3. **Run** the query again.

4. The query displays with four visible fields.

5. **Save** and **close** the query.

A4.3   Creating a Form

A **form** is a database object that is used to enter, edit, and view records. A form displays your data in a more user-friendly format without the columns and rows. Access has several different ways of creating a form. Forms can be created using the Form Wizard (a step-by-step process), using the Form tool, or a self-design. The **Form tool** creates a form that includes all the fields of a table or other database object. A subform is a form that is inserted in another form.

1. With the **National_Ins4** database still open.

2. Click the **Create** tab.

3. Select the **Form Wizard** command in the **Forms** group; a Form Wizard dialog box appears.

4. Click the down arrow of the **Tables/Queries** category and select the **Client_tbl**.

5. Select the [**Client_LName**] under **Available Fields** and click the single arrow (**>**) to have the field name move to the **Selected Fields**, as in Figure 4.6.

6. Repeat step 5 to add the **Client_FName** field.

7. Change the table. (Repeat step 4 to change the table.) Choose the **Optional_Life_tbl** and select the following **Available** Fields: **Life_Policy#, Policy_date, Premium_amount.**

8. Click **next**. (three times).

9. Title the form Client_Form and the subform, Optional_life_subform.

10. Click **finish**.

11. **Continue**.

Figure 4.6   Form Wizard

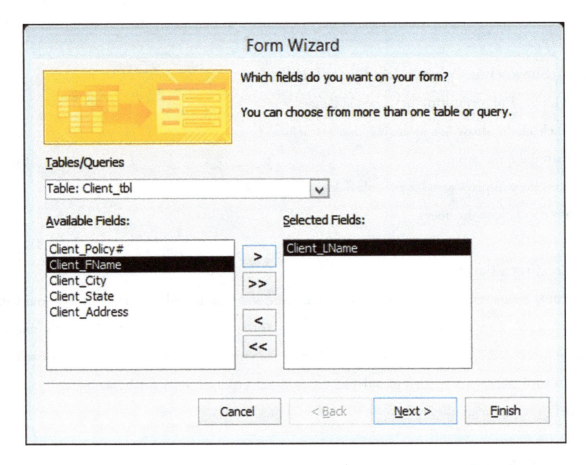

A4.3.1   Modifying a Form

When working with forms, there are many changes that you may want to make such as adjustments to the title of the form, size of the text box, label, and many others. Modifying the structure of a form can be done in Design view. Changes to the layout and design of a form can be made in Layout view. In layout view, changes made are seen immediately. Form view is a non-editing view and is only used to view the form and enter data.

Navigating the form is much like navigating in a table. The record indicator at the bottom of the form shows arrows for next, last, and blank record entry. To navigate through the form fields, click the tab from the keyboard.

A form is designed with many objects that are referred to as **controls**. The fields from a table include a label control and a text box control. The label is placed first in a form with the text box beside it. The label control shows the field name, and the text box control holds the data entered into the field.

Resizing Form Objects

1. Open the **National_Ins4 database.**
2. Open the **Client_Form.**
3. Click the down arrow for the **View** command in the **Views** group and select **layout view**.
4. Resize and line up the **Optional_Life_SubForm** under the title as needed. **Note**: to change and move text boxes, select the text box and move the mouse to the right, near the border of the text box, until the mouse appears as a double-headed arrow. Click, hold, and drag text box to desired position

❖ To select more than one object, hold down the shift key while selecting each of the text box control objects.

A4.3.2 Formatting a Form and Inserting an Image

Formatting can be done to brighten up a form with a logo, an image, and the background color or font color.

1. Select all objects on the form.
2. Click on the **Format** tab of the **Form Layout Tools** contextual tab.
3. Apply bold (**B**) formatting in the **Font** group.
4. Deselect objects by clicking away from the objects.
5. Click the **Design** tab of the **Form Layout Tools.**
6. Click the down arrow for the **Insert Image** command in the **Controls** group.
7. Select **browse** to locate and insert the image from your Access_4 resource folder.
8. Click **OK** to close the **insert picture** dialog box. (The mouse will appear as a rectangle showing an image inside with a plus sign attached to it).

9. Click on the form to insert the image, then resize to the desired position.

10. View the changes in **Form view**.

Change Title on a Form

The form title does not have to remain the same as the form name in the database.

1. With **layout** view of the **Client_Form** selected.

2. Select the title **Client_Form**.

3. Rename the title to **Optional Life,** as shown in Figure 4.7.

4. Review the changes. (Modify the form to your preference.)

5. **Continue**.

Figure 4.7   Modifying a Form

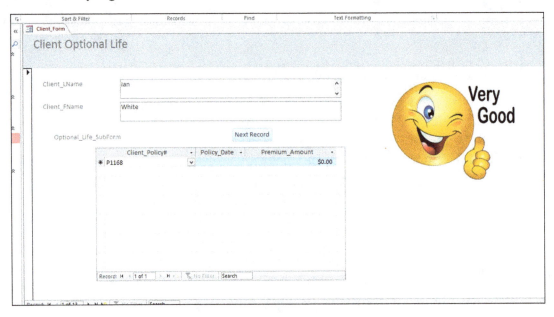

A4.3.3   Add a Control Object to a Form

Some control objects can be added in layout view, while others work better when they are added in design view. In this exercise, we will add a control object to the form.

1. With the **Client_Form open** in **design view.**

2. Click the **Design** tab on the **Form Design Tools** contextual tab.

3. Make sure **Use Control Wizards** command is selected by clicking the **More** down arrow in the **Controls** group and select Use Control Wizards.

4. Next, select the **Button** command in the **Controls** group. The mouse will appear as a white rectangle with a plus sign attached to it.

Step 4   Adding a Control

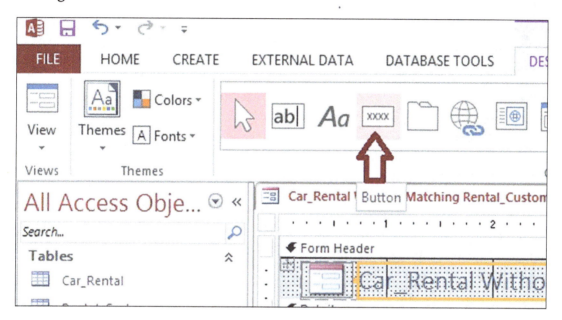

5. Click on the form to have the object inserted. A **Command Button Wizard** dialog box opens.

6. Select **Go To Next Record** from the **Actions** column, as shown in Figure 4.8.

7. Click **next**.

8. Select the **Text** button.

9. Click **next**.

10. Type *Next Record.*

11. Click **finish**.

12. Switch to form view to see results.

Figure 4.8   Command Wizard

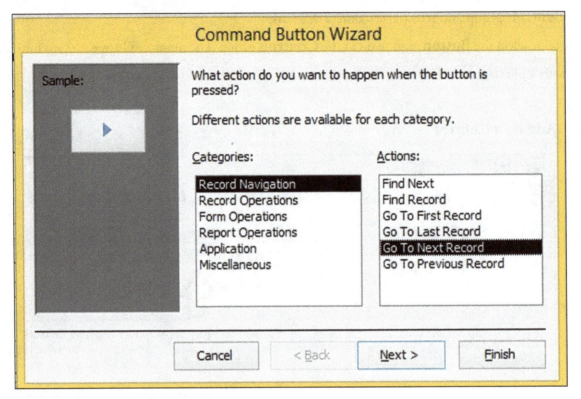

A4.3.4   Printing a Selected Record from a Form

1. Open the **Client_Form** with the desired record selected for printing.

2. Click the **file** tab.

3. Select the **print** tab and choose print.

4. Choose to print either from the **pages** selection or from the **selected** records.

5. Click **OK.**

6. Close table.

Step 4   Print Selected Record

A4.4   Creating a Split Form

A split form gives two views of the same form; the top half displays the form in form view with the bottom portion of the form displaying datasheet view. Both views are synchronized. Records can be entered from either view.

1. With the **National_Ins4** database still open,
2. Select the **client_tbl**.
3. Click the **create** tab and pull the down arrow for the **More Forms** command in the **Forms** group.
4. Select the **Split Form. (Note: t**he **form** opens in layout view.)
5. Select the title of the form and rename it **National Insurance Clients**.
6. **Save** the form as **Client_SForm.**
7. **Continue.**

A4.4.1   Sorting Data in a Form

8. Click in the **Client_LName** field of the form.

9. From the **Home** tab, click **Descending** in the **Sort & Filter** group.

❖ **Note** the records both in the **datasheet view** and those in the **form view** of the **split form** were sorted.

10. **Close** form.

A4.5   Creating a Report using the Report Tool

A **Report** is another Access object that displays the database information in a format for printing. Creating Reports are similar to creating forms. A report can be created with the Report Wizard, the Report tool, or a self-design.

The report has object controls like those in a form, a label control as well as a text box control. Report view, Print preview, Layout view, and Design view are ways to view and modify the report.

1. With the **National_Ins4** database still open,
2. Select the **Optional_Life_tbl**.
3. Click the **create** tab.
4. Select the **Report** command in the **Reports** group. (**Notice**: the report opens in **layout view**).

Step 4   Report Command

Resizing Columns and Renaming the Report Title

5. Resize the columns to fit on one page.

6. Click, hold and drag the horizontal arrows to expand the size of the column. (Notice the entire row is resized.).

7. **Rename** the report title **Life Report**. See Figure 4.9.

Previewing and Saving the Report

8. Switch to **Print Preview** to verify that the report fits on one page. **Notice** the **Print** tab is also located on the **Print Preview** tab.

9. **Save** and title the report: **Client_Life_Report**.

10. **Close** the database.

Figure 4.9   Life Report

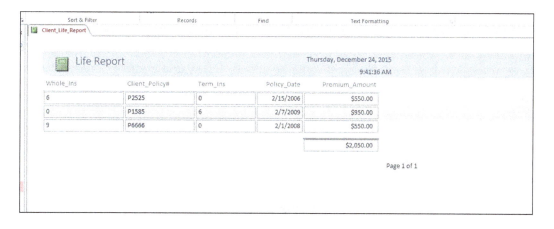

Section 5   Analyzing Data and Performing Calculations

Student Resource folder—(Access_5)

Not only can queries analyze the data in your table, but it can also perform calculations based on aggregate functions using a field value in the table. Adding a label control to a form or report can also be used to perform aggregate function calculations.

I.   **Add a Calculated Control to a Report in Design View**

II. **Apply Functions in a Query to Perform Statistical Calculations**

III. **Create a Crosstab Query**

IV. **Create a Find Duplicates Query**

V.   **Create a Find Unmatched Query**

A5.1   Add a Calculated Control to a Report in Design View

Label controls are objects that are not bound to a field in the table or query however, they can be added to a form/report to perform calculations or provide instructions for the user. In order to add a calculated control object to the report, a text box control object must be added. Calculated control objects placed on a form/report are not stored like fields; instead, the results of the calculated field are calculated each time the form/report is opened. In order to add a calculated field, switch to Design view.

1. Open the **Client_Premium_Report** in the National_Ins5 database.
2. Switch to **Design** view, and extend the **Report Footer.**
3. With the **Report Design Tools** contextual tab in view, make sure the **Design** tab is selected.
4. Select the **Text** box command in the **Controls** group.
5. Click (in the **Report Footer** section of the Report), hold, and drag the mouse pointer to draw a text box.
6. Click inside the unbound text box control.
7. Type **=Sum([PremiumAmount]). Hint**: Mathematical expressions can be entered in a text box control, but it must begin with an equal (**=**) sign, and field names are enclosed in square brackets, as shown in Figure 5.1. Note: formulas follow the same rule as Excel, no spaces.
8. Double click the label control object adjacent to the calculated text box control that displays [**Text##**]. (**Note** the ## is just a number for the label object.)
9. Replace the [Text##] with [**Total**]. **Note:** the width of the box increases as you type the text.

Figure 5.1   Calculated Report

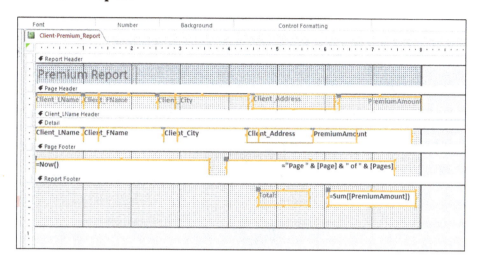

10. In form view, the object displays the calculated value.

11. With the calculated control object still selected (In design view),

12. Select the **Property Sheet** command in the **Tools** group and click the **Format** tab.

13. Click the down-pointing arrow and select **Currency** from the drop-down list, as shown in Figure 5.2.

14. Close the **Property Sheet** when finished.

Note: you could also select the PremiumAmount in the detail section and select **sum** from the **Totals** command in the **Grouping** & **Totals** group.

Figure 5.2   Property Sheet

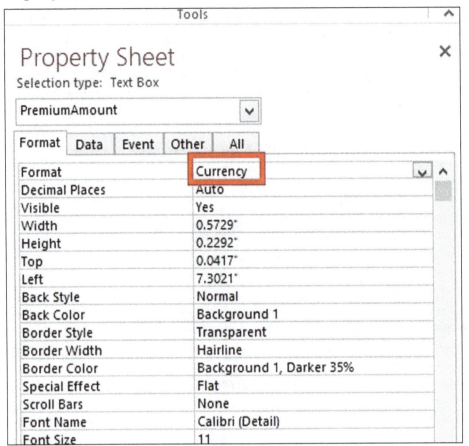

Delete Control Objects

Select the **Client_State** label and text box control object, and click **delete** from the keyboard. Repeat steps to delete the Client_Policy# label and text box control object.

Moving and Aligning a Control Object

1. Switch to layout view and select the Client_Lname, point to the border of the control object until the pointer displays a two-headed arrow, then drag and move the control objects so that all objects align and fit on one page.

    ❖   To **move** one control at a time, select the desired control, select the gray rectangle box handle in the top corner and move to new location.

2. Deselect control.

3. **Save.**

A5.2 Apply Functions in a Query to Perform Statistical Calculations

Aggregate functions perform statistical calculations such as Avg, Min, Max, Count, and Total on records in a table or query. Access will display a row in the query results datasheet, called **Total**, that displays each statistical calculation result. Applying the **Group by Operator** allows each record to be grouped according to the values in the field.

1. Open the **National_Ins5** database.

2. Click the **create** tab.

3. Select the **Query Design** command from the **Queries** group.

4. Select the client_tbl and **add** it to the query design grid. **Close** the **Show Table** dialog box.

5. Double click the client_city field (it will be added to the first column of the design grid).

6. Next, double click **PremiumAmoun**t to add this field in the next three columns, as shown in Figure 53.

7. Click the **Totals** command in the **Show/Hide** group of the **Query Tools** contextual tab. See Figure 5.4.

Figure 5.3   Aggregate Function

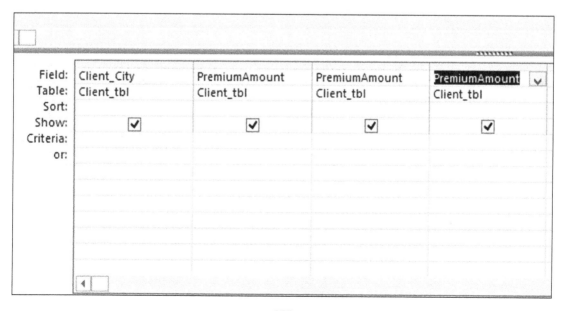

Figure 5.4   Totals Row

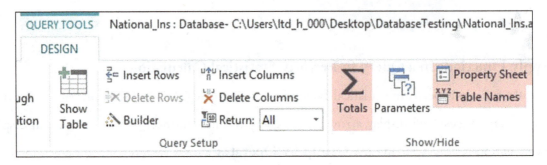

8. Notice a **Total** row was added to the query design grid. The statistics will be calculated by groups; in this case, the statistics will be calculated on the **PremiumAmount** for each city.

9. Click in the **Group By** field of the first (**PremiumAmount**) column and select **Min** from the down-pointing arrow.

10. Select the **Avg** and **Sum** consecutively for the remaining **PremiumAmount** columns. See Figure 5.5.

11. **Run** the query. Compare results to Figure 5.6.

12. **Save** as **StatsByCity_qry**.

13. **Close** query.

Figure 5.5   StatsByCity_Qry

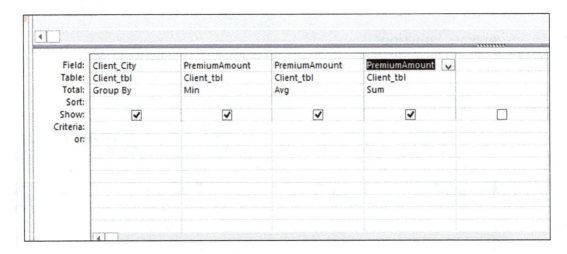

Figure 5.6   Query Results

Client_City	MinOfPremiumAmount	AvgOfPremiumAmount	SumOfPremiumAmount
Augusta	$225.00	$225.00	$225.00
Baltimore	$460.00	$597.33	$1,792.00
Charleston	$720.00	$720.00	$720.00
Greensboro			
Jersey City	$780.00	$780.00	$780.00
Memphis	$350.00	$350.00	$350.00
Miami	$595.00	$645.00	$1,290.00
Portland	$789.00	$789.00	$789.00
San Diego	$475.00	$475.00	$475.00
Seattle	$650.00	$650.00	$650.00

A5.3   Create a Crosstab Query

A **crosstab** query also calculates aggregate functions and groups the results by two sets of values, one for the row headings and the other for the column headings with at least one database field to perform the aggregate function calculation. The wizard guides you through the steps for creating the query.

1. Open the **ZumbaFit** database.
2. Click the **Create** tab and select the **Query Wizard** in the **Queries** group.
3. Select **Crosstab Query** Wizard from the **New Query** dialog box, as shown in Figure 5.7
4. Click **OK**.
5. Click **next** when the **Crosstab Query Wizard** dialog box opens.
6. Select Instructor and click the arrow (**>**) for it to move to the **Selected Fields**.
7. Click **next**.
8. Click ZumbaClass for the column headings.
9. Click **next**.
10. Select **cost** from the field's category on the left and **sum** from the functions category on the right, as shown in Figure 5.8
11. Click **next**.
12. Save the query as **ZumbaZ_Crosstab_qry**.
13. Click **finish**. Notice the crosstab query groups each of the exercise classes by instructor and performs a sum calculation for each of the classes, as shown in Figure 5.9.
14. **Close** the query and the database.

Figure 5.7   Query Design

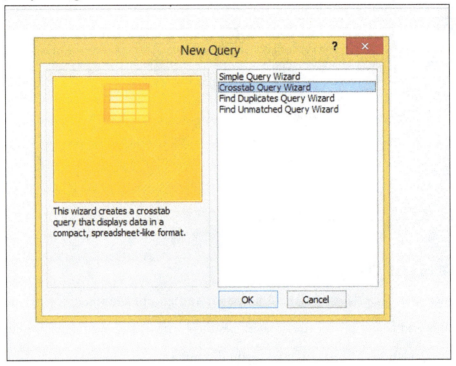

Figure 5.8   Crosstab Query Wizard

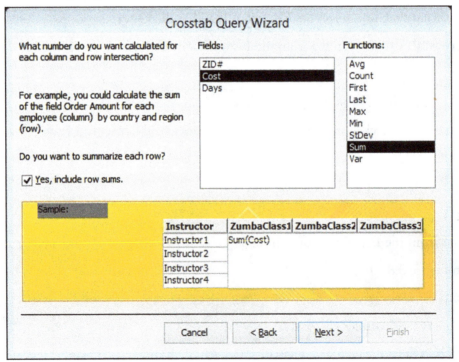

Figure 5.9   Zumba Crosstab Query

Instructor ▾	Total Of Cost ▾	Aqua Zumba ▾	dance ▾	fitness ▾	zumba ▾
Hay	$430.00	$65.00	$150.00	$55.00	$160.00
Julie	$125.00				$125.00
Rachel	$264.00	$75.00	$59.00	$65.00	$65.00
Sarah	$85.00				$85.00

A5.4   Create a Find Duplicates Query

Queries can be created to search and **find duplicate** field values in a table or query. As your database grows, you may want to assure yourself that data has not been duplicated. Consequently, there are other reasons for using a find duplicates query, such as tracking specific repeat customers in one household to save on mailing.

1. Open the **JR_Rentals** Database.

2. Click the create tab.

3. Select the **Query Wizard** command in the **Queries** group.

4. Select the **Find Duplicates Query Wizard.**

5. Click **OK.**

6. From the **Find Duplicates Query Wizard** dialog box, select table: **Rental_Customer,** as shown in Figure 5.10.

7. Click **next**.

8. Select **Fname** and then click the arrow (**>**) to move it over to the **Duplicate-value fields.**

9. Repeat step 8 for **Lname**. See Figure 5.11.

10. Click **next**.

11. Click the double arrow (**>>**) to move all of the remaining fields to the **Additional query fields** on the right.

12. Click **next**.

13. Click **finish**. View the records and compare to Figure 5.12.

> ❖ **Note:** There are two records that were entered twice with inconsistent data.

Figure 5.10   Duplicate Query

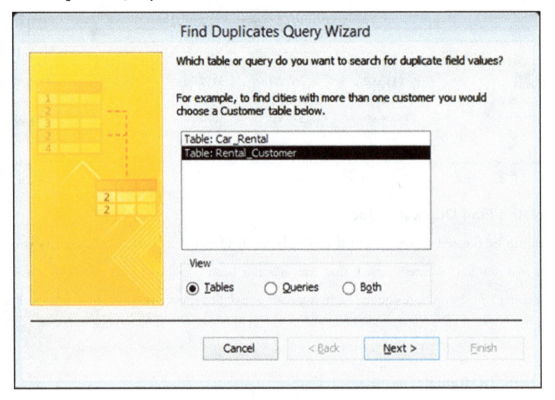

Figure 5.11   Match Duplicate Fields

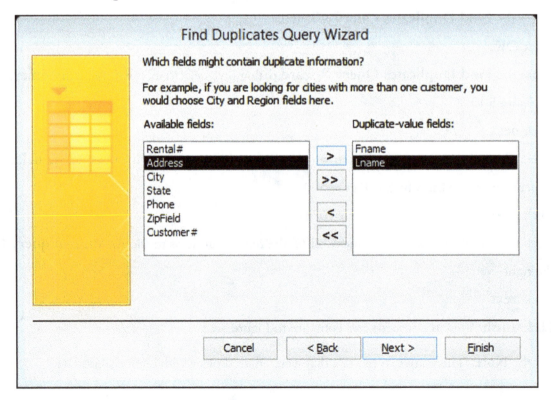

Figure 5.12   Duplicate Query Results

Fname	Lname	Rental#	Address	City	State	Phone	Zip Code	Customer#
Jan	Goetz	R233	1250 Gateway Dr		Seattle	804-132-1725	98109	C3011
Jan	Goetz	R230	17 Chester Ln	Aurora	Miami	630-442-5943	33129	C3005
Samuel	Saul	R234	1325 Monarch Dr		Baltimore	719-652-1325	21206	C3012
Samuel	Saul	R277	17 Gunston Dr		Baltimore	410-610-1238	21215	C3006

A5.5   Create a Find Unmatched Query

This type of query is used when you would like to compare the data between two tables that may have incomplete records in one table or don't have a matching record in the related table. The Query Wizard will guide you through the process to create the select query.

1. Open the **JR_Rentals** Database.
2. Click the **create** tab.
3. Select the **Query Wizard** command in the **Queries** group.
4. Select the **Find Unmatched Query Wizard.**
5. Click **OK.**
6. Make sure the table: **Car_Rental** is selected**.**
7. Click **next.**
8. Click **next again**.
9. The matching field in both tables is the **Rental#** field, and it should be highlighted; see Figure 5.13.
10. Click the matching field button (**< = >**) in the center of the two columns for it to appear in the **Matching fields** box.
11. Click **next.**
12. Select the double arrow (**> >**) to move all of the remaining fields to the **Selected** fields category on the right.
13. Click **next.**
14. Click **finish**.

❖ **Note:** there is one record that has no matching record in the related table, as shown in Figure 5.14.

261

Figure 5.13   Unmatched Query

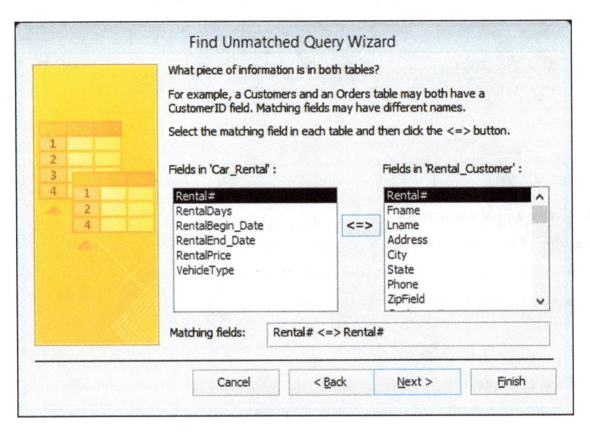

Figure 5.14   Query Results

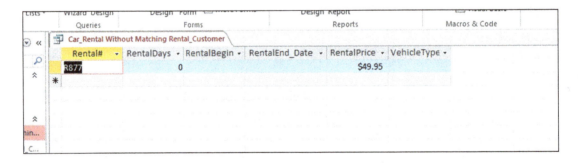

Integrating across Office Applications

Exporting tables from Access to Word or Excel provides flexibility in maintaining your data in other formats.

I. **Export Access into Excel**

II. **Export an Access Table to Word**

III. **Export an Access Report to Word**

[Resource File—Int_1]

Int-1.1   Export Access into Excel

Sharing and exchanging data between Microsoft Access and Microsoft Excel allows you to update and maintain records in one application while linking to another. To export data from Access into Excel:

1. Open the **Faculty** database.
2. Select the **College_Faculty_tbl.**
3. Click the **External Data** tab.,.
4. Select the **Excel** command in the **Export** group. (An **Export Excel Spreadsheet** dialog box opens.) See Figure 1
5. Select the **Browse** button next to the **File name** to locate the Int_1 resource folder.
6. Select the Excel workbook **Linking.xlsx**.
7. Click **save**.
8. Click **OK**.
9. Click **close**.
10. Now open the Excel file, **Linking.xlsx** to view the imported table, as shown in Figure 2.
11. Modify the spreadsheet by expanding the columns to view the data.
12. **Close** the workbook and **close** the database**.**

Figure 1   **Exporting Data**

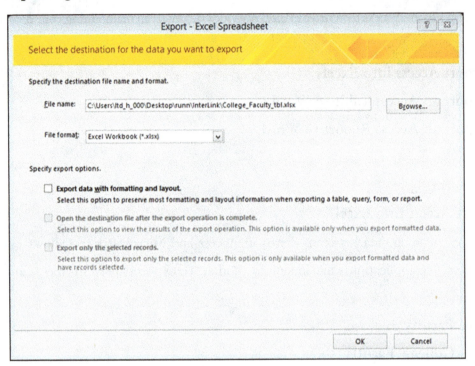

Figure 2   **Exporting Results**

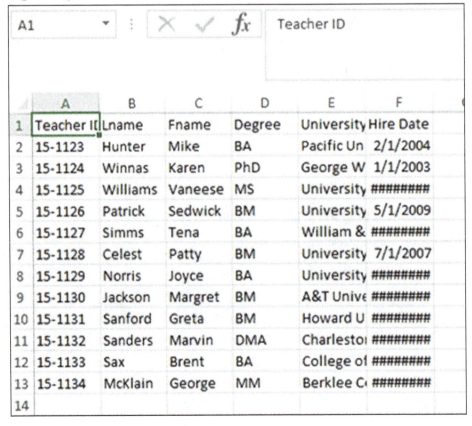

Int-1.2   Export an Access Table to Word

Exporting an Access table to Word is great for inserting data into a Word report or document. The steps are similar to exporting an Access table to Excel except the document is exported as an RTF file, meaning that it is saved in a rich text format. This only means that the formatting is preserved for fonts and styles. **Note**: Changes to the Access table can be made after it is exported to Word.

1. With the **Faculty** database open.
2. Select the **Coverage_tbl.**
3. Click the **External Data** tab.
4. Select the down-pointing arrow for the **more** command in the **Export** group.
5. Select **Word** from the drop-down menu. (An **Export RTF File** dialog box opens).
6. Select the **Browse** button next to the **File name** to locate the Int_1 resource folder.
7. Notice the **file name** is the same as the table name in Access. See Figure 3.
8. Click **save**.
9. Click **OK**.
10. Click **close**.
11. Open the resource folder and view the file **Coverage_tbl.rtf**.
12. **Close** the Word file.
13. **Close** the Access **coverage_tbl**.

Step 4   Export RTF

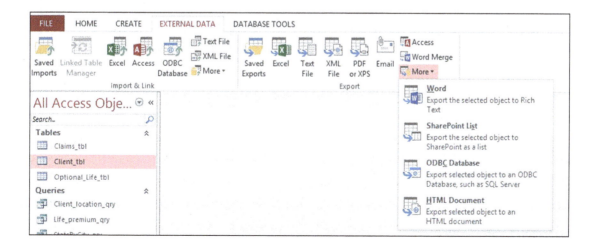

Figure 3   Saving Exported File

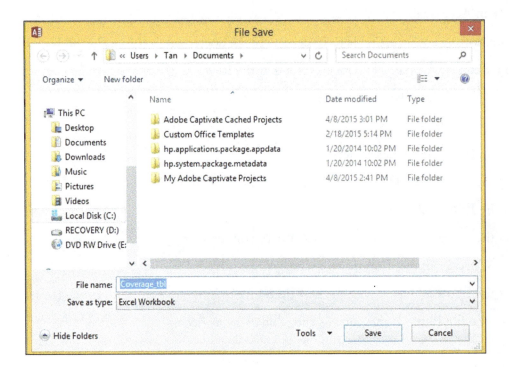

Step 11   Coverage_tbl.rtf

Ins_ID	Teacher ID	Coverage	Dental	Premium	Deductible
C-101	15-1123	HMO	No	420	500
C-102	15-1124	PPO	Yes	580	250
C-103	15-1125	POS	Yes	754	250
C-104	15-1126	HDHP	Yes	2500	1250
C-105	15-1127	HDHP	Yes	1750	2500
C-106	15-1128	PPO	No	575	500
C-107	15-1129	HMO	Yes	750	250
C-108	15-1130	EPO	No	550	500
C-109	15-1131	EPO	Yes	475	500
C-110	15-1132	HMO	No	475	250
C-111	15-1133	HMO	Yes	550	500
C-112	15-1134	POS	No	625	500

Int-1.3   Export an Access Report to Word

The Access Report is exported as an RTF file to preserve the formatting for fonts and styles. However, modifications can be made in Word.

1. Open the **Faculty** database.

2. Select the **Faculty_Report**.

3. Click the **External Data** tab and then click the down-pointing arrow for the **More** command in the **Export** group.

4. Select **Word** from the drop-down menu. (**Notice** the default file name is identical to the report name.

5. Click the **browse** button to locate the destination for the report.

6. Check the box to **open the destination file after the export operation is complete.** (See Figure 4 to view the report.)

7. Click **OK.**

Figure 4   Faculty Report

Teacher ID	Lname	Fname	Degree	University	Hire Date
15-1123	Hunter	Mike	BA	Pacific University	2/1/2004
15-1124	Winnas	Karen	PhD	George Washington	1/1/2003
15-1125	Williams	Vaneese	MS	University of Maryland	3/15/2000
15-1126	Patrick	Sedwick	BM	University of Virgina	5/1/2009
15-1127	Simms	Tena	BA	William & Mary	1/15/2002
15-1128	Celest	Patty	BM	University of Portland	7/1/2007
15-1129	Norris	Joyce	BA	University of Portland	1/25/2004
15-1130	Jackson	Margret	BM	A&T University	8/15/2002
15-1131	Sanford	Greta	BM	Howard University	1/25/2008
15-1132	Sanders	Marvin	DMA	Charleston Southern	1/25/2008
15-1133	Sax	Brent	BA	College of Charleston	1/15/2007
15-1134	McKlain	George	MM	Berklee College of Music	2/15/2003
15-1135	Henry	Joseph	BA	Morehouse College	3/15/2007
15-1136	Johnson	Mary	MA	Kaplan University	1/25/2006
15-1137	Hay	Vermell	MS	Towson University	6/17/2009
15-1138	Justin	Paul	BS	Spellman College	1/15/2010
15-1139	Smith	Sabrina	PhD	George Mason University	1/25/2009

College Faculty — Thursday, December 24, 2015

Index

Access 2015

Knowledge and Skill Assessment

A1   Knowledge Check

1. What is the unique key identifier? _____

2. What dialog box opens when we click on the **more commands** from the **Quick Access Toolbar**? _____

3. To create a **blank new database**, a _____ must be given, and a _____ must be selected for storing the database.

4. _____ is a software application that is designed to retrieve, modify, or maintain related information.

5. The___ _____ displays the name of the document and the name of the application.

6. The _____ ___ _____ gives you quick access to regularly common tasks.

7. The _____ displays information about the database.

A2   Knowledge Check

1. The collection of fields related to one unit of information is known as a _____.

2. _____ is the process of copying the database to protect information from loss or damage.

3. The collection of related records make up the _____.

4. The _____ determines what types of values or information can be entered into a field.

5. A collection of related tables is called a _____.

6. _____ is a system that rearranges the data and the objects in the database to decrease its file size, which gives you more disk space.

7. A _____ field is a field that appears in both tables.

A3   Knowledge Check

1. There are two views to create tables in Access, datasheet view and _____ view.

2. The field size property is used to set the number of _____ allowed in a field.

3. An _____ _____displays data in a specific pattern, making data easier to read.

4. A _____ _____field restricts the data that is entered into a field.

5. _____ _____ are created to avoid the user data entry errors.

6. In a **one-to-many** relationship, the table that is referred to as the **one** is considered the _____table and the table that is referred to as the **many** is considered the _____ table.

7. The rules that govern and enforce the consistency of the database is called_____ _____.

A4   Knowledge Check

1. The object in a database that create printouts in hard copy format is called a _____.

2. A _____is an object that extracts data from the database to answer specific questions about the data stored in the database.

3. The results of a query display your answers in records called a _____.

4. A _____ is a database object that is used to enter, edit, and view records.

5. Queries can perform calculations? True/False

6. A _____form gives two views of a form.

7. The label control shows the field name, and the text box control holds the data entered into the field? True/False

A5   Knowledge Check

1. ____ _____ are objects that are not bound to a field in a table or query, and it can also be added to a form for instructions or calculations.

2. _____functions can be used to perform statistical calculations.

3. Mathematical expressions can be entered in a text box control of a Report? True/False

4. A _____ query can be used to find duplicate records in a table.

5. _____query is used to find records that may not have matching records in a related table.

6. A ____ ____ ____object can be used to enter a mathematical expression in a Report.

7. The format tab of the ____ ____ is where the currency can be applied to a calculated control.

Skill Assessments 1 and 2

Creating a Database through Internet Research

1. Select five to seven television shows that aired in 2014 that you found to be your top TV shows of all times. View the information below for planning your database.

2. Create a new blank database and title it **TV_Shows**.

3. Create a table and title it **Top2014**. Include the following information:

    a. Primary Key (optional) (**Hint**: Primary Key can always be the default value.)

    b. Best_TV_Shows   e.   Network

    c. Main_Char   f.   Support_Char

    d. Rating   g.   Season

4. **Sort** the Best_TV_Shows in ascending order.

5. **Save** and **close** the table.

6. **Close** the database.

Skill Assessment 3

Modify a Table in Design View

[Student Resource File—SkillAssessment_3]

1. Open the **DynastyEnterprise** database.

2. Create a one-to-many relationship between the **Rep_tbl** (primary table) and the **Dynasty_Realty** table (related table) with the common field: RepID#.

3. Modify the Rep_tbl with the following information:

    a. Add a **BidAmount** field with currency data type.

    b. Put an Input Mask on the **Cell#** field.

    c. Create a Lookup Field for the **State** field and choose the option to have the lookup field get the values from the State_tbl. (**Note**: say yes to the field size change).

    d. Create a validation rule for the **BidAmount** field for >750000. Enter appropriate text for the validation text message.

4. Modify the following records in the **Rep_tbl** with the information from Table 3–1 below. You choose the BidAmount for each record to comply with the validation rule.

Table 3–1   Table Data

RepID#	RepName	Cell#	State	BidAmount
R501	Thompson	703-682-5565	VA	800,000
R526	Baker	253-781-1325	WA	790,000
R580	Wright	704-253-1786	NC	850,000

5. Sort the **RepName** field in descending order.

6. **Close** the table.

7. **Compact** the database.

8. **Close** the database.

Skill Assessment 4

Create a Calculated Field in a Query, Add a Criteria to a Query

[Student Resource File—SkillAssessment_4]

1. Open the **VAtlantic_Insurance4** database.

2. Create a query with the Query Wizard with fields from the Insurance_tbl and the Client_tbl. Include the following fields.

Client_tbl	Insurance_tbl
Fname	Paid
Lname	Monthly_Premium

3. Save the query as LateFee_qry.

4. View the query in the recordset and switch to Design view.

5. Add a **criteria** to view only unpaid clients.

6. Add a **calculated field** for the Monthly_Premium. Multiply the Monthly_Premium by 1% and label the new column *Late Fee:*

7. Format the calculated field as currency.

8. Save and run the query.

9. Create a **form** for the Client_tbl using the Form command.

10. Modify the form with the following:

a. Title the form **Client Information**.

b. Bold the text.

c. Change the font size to 18.

11. **Save** the form as **Client_frm**.

12. **Close** the form.

Skill Assessment 5

Adding a Calculated Field to a Report, Find Unmatched and Find Duplicates Query, Create a Crosstab Query

[Student Resource File—SkillAssessment_5]

1. Open the **VAtlantic_Insurance5** database.

2. Create a **crosstab query** that summarizes the Insurance Reps monthly insurance payments by insurance codes. Choose the following information to create the query.

a. Select the Insurance_tbl.

b. Make the InsuranceRep the row heading.

c. Make the Insurance_Code the column heading.

d. Sum the Monthly_Premium.

e. Title the crosstab query: Rep_Premium.

3. **Save** and run query. (Adjust columns if needed.)

4. **Close** query.

5. Select the **Find Unmatched Query Wizard** to compare the Client_tbl with the Insurance_tbl for missing information. Determine the relevant fields to display. Title the query: Unmatched_Client_info_qry.

6. **Close** the Unmatched query.

7. Select the **Find Duplicates Query Wizard** to analyze the Client_tbl to search for records of clients in the same household. Determine the relevant fields and display the remaining fields in the query recordset. Title the query Duplicate_Client_info_qry.

8. Open the LateFee_Report.

9. Modify the report with the following:

a. Create a calculated control object to the right of the Monthly_Premium total that will add the sum of the Monthly_Premium fee, of 1% for unpaid clients.

b. Format the control object for Currency.

c. Bold the amounts.

d. Change the report title to Late Fee Report and apply **bold** formatting.

e. Adjust the columns to fit on one page in Landscape.

f. Close the report.

10. Create a new report with the Report Wizard based on the Client_tbl. Modify the report as follows:

a. Change the report title to VAtlantic Clients.

b. Change the font size to 18.

c. Bold the text.

d. Adjust all field columns to fit on one page in Landscape.

e. Print Preview the Report.

f. Save report as Client_Report.

g. Close report and Database.

Answer Key

Answers A1

1. Primary key
2. Access Options
3. Filename, location
4. Access
5. Title bar
6. Quick Access Toolbar
7. Status bar

Answers A2

1. Record
2. Backup
3. Table
4. Data type
5. Relational Database
6. Compacting
7. Common

Answers A3

1. Design
2. Characters
3. Input Mask
4. Lookup column
5. Validation Rules
6. Primary, Related
7. Referential Integrity

Answers A4

1. Report
2. Query
3. Recordset
4. Form
5. True
6. Split
7. True

Answers A5

1. Label control
2. Aggregate
3. True
4. Duplicate
5. Unmatched
6. Text box control
7. Property sheet

PowerPoint 2013

PowerPoint is a presentation software application that can be used for many different purposes. With the advancement of technology, employers have high expectations for seeking the best possible candidates to employ. With that said, interviewing for jobs have now become very competitive, and applicants must compete for jobs through performance-based interviews, projects, and even presentations.

Presentations can include different types of graphics or forms of multimedia. PowerPoint presentations can be viewed through a personal computer network or shared over a network for work or school.

This tutorial will help to improve your skills, knowledge, and abilities with the PowerPoint application. Exercises are performance-based drills for skill development. Lessons are designed to guide you through the essentials and then introduce you to some advanced concepts that are relevant to the workforce.

PowerPoint 2013

Section I   PowerPoint Essentials

I.   Opening a Blank PowerPoint Presentation

II. Identifying the PowerPoint Graphical User Interface—(GUI)

III. Exploring the Ribbon

IV. Customizing the Quick Access Toolbar

V.   PowerPoint Help Feature

VI. Navigating in PowerPoint

P1.1   Opening a Blank PowerPoint Presentation

To get started working in PowerPoint creating presentations, you need to open a blank presentation.

1. From the **Start Screen,** tap or click the start screen button in the lower left corner of the screen.

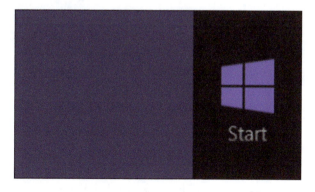

2. Begin typing PowerPoint. The search panel will open.

3. Select the **Blank Presentation,** as shown in Figure 1.1

4. A **blank** presentation opens.

5. Continue.

Figure 1.1   Blank Presentation

P1.2   Identifying PowerPoint Graphical User Interface (GUI)

Explore the **PowerPoint** interface to become familiar with the new features and the changes for improving your presentation experience.

Compare and contrast the screen in Figure 1.2 with your screen.

Refer to Table 1.1 for a Description of PowerPoint Features.

Figure 1.2   GUI

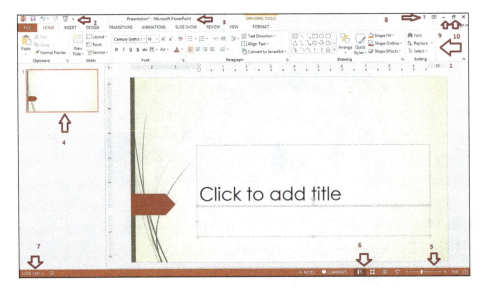

Table 1.1   Features and Description

Indicator	Features	Description
1	Ribbon	Tabs are on top. Groups are on bottom and commands are in between.
2	Quick Access Toolbar	Common tasks button
3	Title Bar	Shows name of document and application name.
4	Slides Pane	Miniature slides pane with content viewing. Outline display.
5	Zoom Indicator	Zooms in or out of document.
6	Slide views	Document viewing adjustment
7	Status bar	Displays document information (pages, word count. Right click the status bar to customize.
8	Help Feature	Provides resources such as videos, tutorials, and online assistance.
9	Minimize button	Minimize the screen
10	Restore button	Restores the screen
	Vertical scroll	Slides up or down. Default settings can be changed through the advanced options menu.

P1.3   Exploring the Ribbon

The **Ribbon** is designed with **Tab** buttons on top and **Group** associated buttons on the bottom. These commands allow you access to **PowerPoint's** common tasks. There is an option to view or hide the ribbon; see Figure 1.3. The file tab is referred to as the **backstage view**, and it is where you customize your personal tab and group commands.

Note: Contextual Tabs are also displayed on the ribbon. However, **contextual tabs** only appear when an object is selected to give further command options for working with that particular object.

To customize the tabs on the Ribbon:

1. Click the **file** tab to access the **backstage view,** as shown in Figure 1.4.
2. Click **Options** from the navigation pane.

Figure 1.3   **Show/Hide Ribbon**

Figure 1.4   **File Tab**

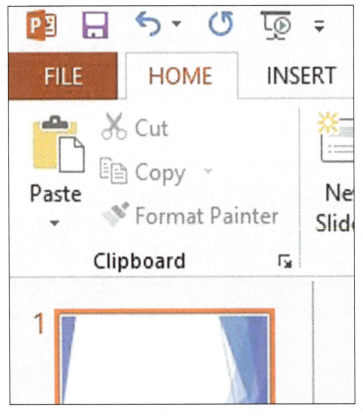

3. Click the **Customize Ribbon** command from the categories on the left.

4. On the right, under **customize the ribbon**, click **new tab** at the bottom of the dialog box, as shown in Figure 1.5.

❖ **Note:** the new tab and new group appears together as a set.

5. Make sure **new tab** is selected; then click **rename**. Enter a name for the new tab.

6. Next, select **new group** and click the **rename** tab to give the new group a name of your choice. A **rename** dialog box will open with an *option* to choose an image.

7. With your new group selected, choose your group-associated commands. (These are the commands that you use regularly such as the font, font size, the format painter, paste. . . .)

8. Select your commands from the choices on the left and **add** them to your new group on the right.

9. Click **OK** when finished.

Figure 1.5   Customizing Tabs

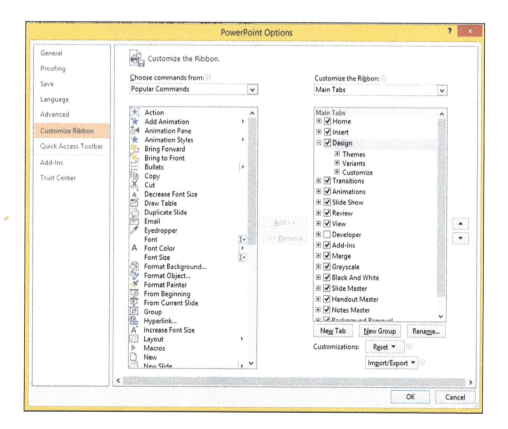

P1.4 Customizing the Quick Access Toolbar

The **Quick Access Toolbar** allows you to add commands that you access on a daily basis much quicker. The **Quick Access Toolbar** is located either above or below the ribbon.

1. Click the drop-down arrow to the right of the **Quick Access Toolbar**, depending on the location. See Figure 1.6.

2. Select the commands that you wish to have added to your **Quick Access Toolbar.**

❖ In order to choose more commands, click the **More Commands** option to add more items to your Quick Access Toolbar.

Figure 1.6   Customizing Quick Access Toolbar

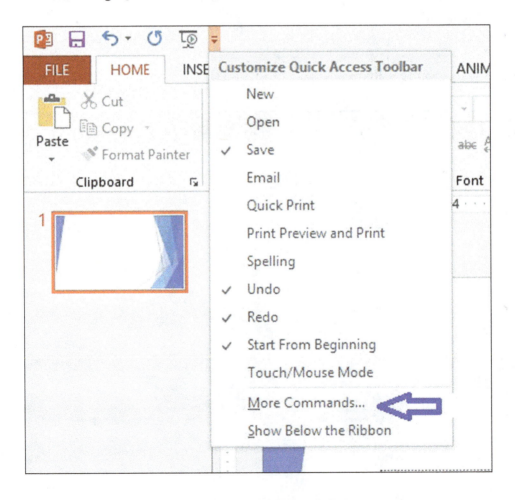

P1.5 PowerPoint Help Feature

The **help** feature displays information on **PowerPoint**. Click the question mark **[?]** that is located in the top right corner of the screen. Enter a word or phrase to search and a list of topics will be displayed.

You can also access the help options by pressing **F1** on your keyboard.

P1.6 Navigating in PowerPoint

1. In **slide show view**, you can advance to the next slide by clicking the mouse, pressing enter from the keyboard, and by using the **up** and **down** arrows on your keyboard to move **forward** and **reverse** through a presentation.

2. In **slide show view**, you may also advance to the next slide by using the navigation buttons in the bottom left corner of your slide.

❖ In **normal view**, slides can be advanced manually by clicking the **previous** and **next** slide navigation arrows.

Step 2 Slide Advancement

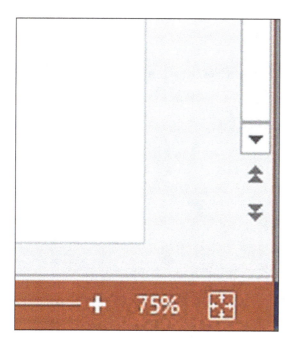

3. To **end** the presentation or stop, click **ESC** from the keyboard.

Section 2   Creating a PowerPoint Presentation

[Resource Folder—(PowerPoint_P2)]

P2.1   Opening a New Presentation

To access a new presentation from the desktop:

1. Click the **File** tab.
2. Select **New** from the navigation bar on the left.
3. Choose a **Design** for your presentation or click **Blank Presentation**.
4. A **new** presentation will appear.

P2.2   Opening an Existing PowerPoint Presentation

To open an **existing** presentation:

1. Select the **File** tab.
2. Select the **Open** tab from the navigation on the left, as shown in Figure 2.1.
3. Select **computer** then **browse** for the location of the PowerPoint file; the **open** dialog box will appear.
4. Select your presentation.
5. Click **Open.**

❖ For presentations that were recently opened, browse the **Recent Presentations** to search for files instead of browsing through your computer files.

Figure 2.1   Recent Presentation

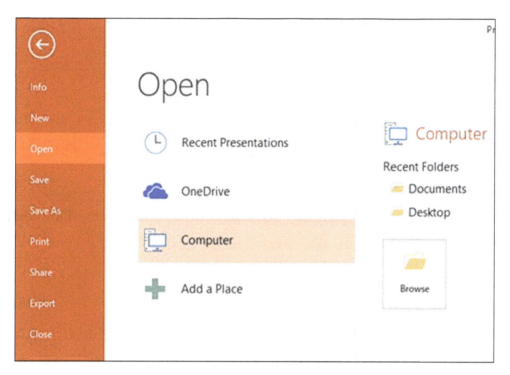

P2.3   Working with PowerPoint Templates

Templates are predesigned presentations that have a variety of different styles, custom formatting, and design themes, which will save you time from creating your own.

1. Click the **File** tab and select **New.**
2. Choose a **template.** (You can choose from the **Suggested searches** or enter a **search** of your own for specific **template** types.)
3. **Preview** templates.
4. Click **create** to download the desired template.

Step 4   Create Template

P2.4   Inserting/Deleting Slides

A new PowerPoint presentation opens with one slide inserted by default: the **Title Slide.** Additional slides can be inserted with a selection of slide layouts to choose from.

1. Open a **blank** presentation.
2. Click the down-pointing arrow next to the **New Slide** command.
3. Choose your desired slide presentation layout.
4. Left click once and the slide will be inserted into the presentation. (Repeat to add additional slides.)
5. Click the text placeholder and begin typing to add text to the slide.

Step 2   New Slide

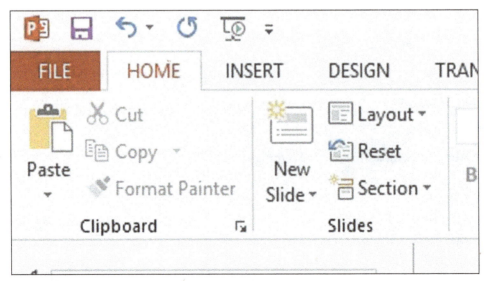

P2.4.1 Deleting Slides

1. Select the **title** slide for deletion.

2. Click **delete** from the keyboard.

3. Slide will be removed from the presentation.

4. **Close** without saving.

P2.5 Adding Transition to Slides

Adding **transition** to a slide can effectively enhance the presentation for your viewers. **Transition** is the grand entrance of a slide show, and it captures the attention of your audience. PowerPoint has some very impressive slide transitions to fit any purpose. Slide transitions are animated, and the animations range from simple to complex features.

1. Open the **Higher Standards** presentation.

2. Select the **slide #1** for transition.

3. Select the **Transition** tab and click the **more** commands down- arrow located in the **Transition to This Slide** group to select the **Vortex** transition from the **Exciting** category selection.

Step 3 More Command Options

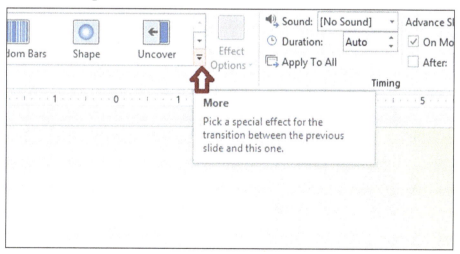

4. Select **slide #2** and choose a different transition.

5. To preview slide transitions, select the **Transition** tab and choose the **Preview** command from the **Preview** group.

6. **Save** and continue.

Step 5   Transitions

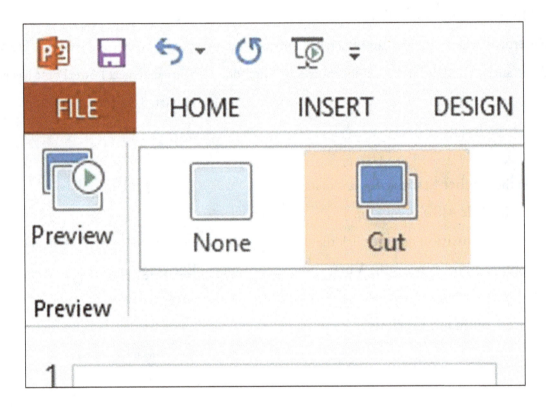

P2.6   Choosing a Design Theme

Presentation **Design** Themes are predefined formats that include a pattern and color scheme for fonts, slide layouts, and effects. These designs can be modified and saved for repeated use. **Theme Designs** bring a look of professional excellence and consistency to a presentation if applied properly.

1. With the **Higher Standards** presentation open, select the **Design** tab.

2. Select the **more** commands down- arrow that is located in the **themes** group (to access more themes).

3. Choose the **Berlin** design **theme**.

4. **Save** work.

P2.7   Running a PowerPoint Presentation

PowerPoint presentations can advance manually or automatically through a slide show. Microsoft offers several different options to present or **share** your presentation, including **email**, **One Drive**, or online through the **Office Presentation Service**, which is a free public service that allows others to view your presentation through a web browser. The **Share** commands and options are available **backstage**.

Presenting a Slide Show Manually

1. With the **Higher Standards** presentation still open,
2. Click the **Slide-Show** tab.
3. Select, **From Beginning,** located in the **Start Slide Show** group.

Presenting a Slide Show Automatically

To have the slide show advance **automatically** through the presentation, **timing** must be applied to each individual slide. This allows each slide to be displayed for a specific length of time, and the presentation will run hands-free.

1. With **Higher Standards** still selected, select **slide #2**.
2. Select the **Transitions** tab.
3. Uncheck the box, **On Mouse Click** located in the **timing** group**.**
4. In the **After** field, enter 00:01.30 seconds.
5. Select next slide and enter 00:01.40 seconds. Set the same timing for the remaining slides.
6. **Run** the presentation **From Beginning**.
7. **Save** and continue.

Rehearse Timings

When preparing a presentation, the **Rehearse Timings** command lets you prepare for your presentation and **set** actual timing for each slide while you practice speaking.

It is wise to always rehearse your presentation before presenting it to an audience.

1. With the **Higher Standards** still selected,
2. Click the **Slide Show** tab.

3. Choose the **Rehearse Timings** command from the **Set Up** group.

4. **Rehearse Timings** will begin recording immediately, so practice your presentation!

P2.8   Saving a Presentation

When documents are created, you will need to save it initially for later retrieval. PowerPoint offers two options for saving presentation files: the **Save** and **Save As** options.

Save As: this option should be used to initially save a PowerPoint file, make a copy of an original file, or for renaming a presentation document.

1. Click the **File** tab.
2. Select the **Save As** command.
3. Click **computer;** then **browse** to choose the location to save the presentation document, as shown in Figure 2.2.
4. With the **Save As** dialog box open, select the desired location to store the presentation and give it a **file name.**
5. Click the **save** button.

Save: This option should be used after the presentation has been initially saved. **Save** is located on the **Quick Access Toolbar,** as shown in Figure 2.3. As the workbook is edited and modified, **save** often so that changes made to the workbook are updated.

Note: Other options for saving include saving to the **Cloud** with Microsoft's **One Drive**, saving to an external drive, or saving to your computer drive.

Figure 2.2   Save as

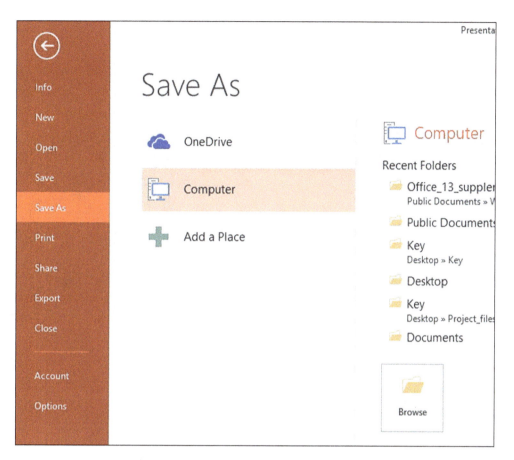

Figure 2.3   **Quick Access Toolbar**

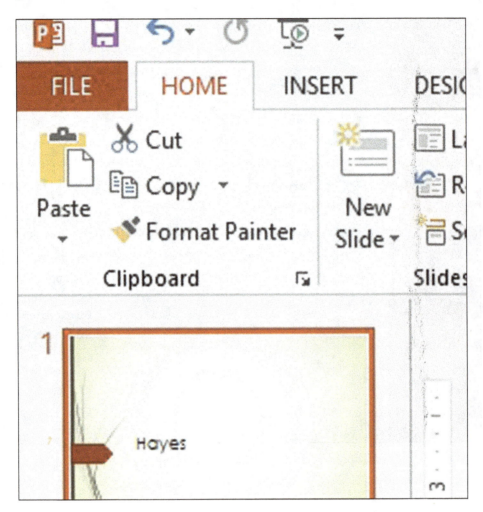

P2.9   Printing in PowerPoint

PowerPoint offers several options for printing your presentation, this includes **handouts** for your audience, a speaker **Notes Page**, an **Outline** format, or **Full Slide** views. Printing handouts for your audience is a good way to provide copies of your presentation.

1. Click the **File** tab.
2. Select the **Print** command from the navigation on the left.
3. Under the **Settings** menu, click the down arrow of the **Full Page Slides** selection. See Figure 2.4. (A menu selection will appear for you to choose your **Print Layout** and **Handout** format.)
4. Choose your desired **print selection** and a **preview** will appear in the **preview window** to the right.
5. Click to **print** selection.

Figure 2.4   Print Settings

P2.9.1   Outline View

1. With the **Higher Standards** presentation open, click on the **View** tab.

2. Select the **Outline View** command in the **Presentation Views** group.

3. An **outline** view of the presentation will appear in the slide navigation pane. (**Note**: Editing can be done in this view.)

Step 3   Outline View

```
1 [ ]  PREPARING FOR WORK
       EMPLOYERS SEEK....

2 [ ]  RESPONDING TO JOB ADS
         • Send Cover Letter
             • Brief – (appetizer)
         • Send Updated Resume
             • Spell check
             • Relevant
             • Verbs/ Tense agreement
             • (Past tense) – past jobs...
         • References
             • If requested

3 [ ]  PREPARING FOR INTERVIEW
         • Research organization
```

P2.10   Closing/Exiting Presentation

To **close** the PowerPoint application:

1. Click the **File** tab.
2. Select **Close** from the navigation pane on the left.
3. The current application will **close**.

❖ Alternately, you can click the **X** in the top corner of the screen to **exit** the presentation. Say yes, if prompted to save.

Section 3   Formatting and Modifying a Presentation

   I.   **Formatting Text**

   II.   **Copying/Pasting Text**

   III. **Find/Replace**

   IV. **Text Alignment and Spacing**

   V.   **Animating Text and Objects**

   VI. **Presentation Views**

   VII. **Spell Check**

Student Resource Folder—(PowerPoint_P3)

P3.1   Formatting Text

Changing the format of your text brings focus and emphasis to major points that are being presented in your presentation.

1. Open the **Purpose** presentation.
2. Select **Title** Text in **slide #1**.
3. From the **Home** tab, select the down arrow for the **Font Color** in the **Font** group.
4. Select **Light Yellow, Text 2.**
5. Select **Text Shadow** and **Bold** from the **Font** group. Click outside of the text box to deselect it.
6. **Save** file.

P3.1.1   Copying Formatting with the Format Painter

1. With **Purpose** still open,
2. Select **Title Text** in **slide #1**.
3. Click on the **Format Painter** in the **Clipboard** group of the **Home** tab. (Notice the mouse resembles the look of a brush.)
4. Scroll down to slide #2 and **brush** across the **Title** with the **Format Painter. (Note:** slide #2 has the same formatting as slide #1.)
5. Repeat **steps 2–4** to apply the same formatting to the remaining **titles** for each slide in the presentation.
6. **Save** file.

Step 3   Format Painter

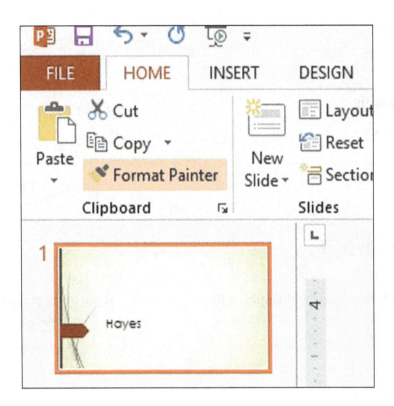

P3.2   Copying/Pasting, Deleting Text

Copying text from one slide to another

1. With **Purpose** still open,

2. Select **slide #5**.

3. Select the subbulleted text: **Handouts**.

4. Click the **Copy** command in the **Clipboard** group of the **Home** tab.

5. Click on **slide #3.** Place the insertion point after the word (**Notes**) and press enter from the keyboard.

6. Click **Paste** in the **Clipboard** group of the **Home** tab.

7. The **new Slide #3** should include a new subbullet for **Handouts**.

8. **Continue.**

To delete text

1. Select **slide #5**.

2. Highlight the last bullet and subbullet that reads: **Determine other outputs needed . . . Handouts**.

3. Press **Delete** from the keyboard to delete the entire bullet and subbullet.

4. **Save** file.

P3.3   Find/Replace

Finding text in a lengthy presentation can become tedious. Therefore, applying the **Find/Replace** command will help to scan the document quicker for words and phrases.

Finding Content

1. With **Purpose** still open,
2. Click the **Find** command in the **Editing** group of the **Home** tab.
3. Select **find** from the drop-down list. (A **Find** dialog box will appear.)
4. Type *Evidence.*
5. Click **Find Next** to scroll through each occurrence of the term.
6. Continue.

Step 2   Find Command

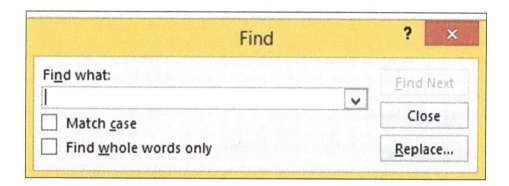

Replacing Content

1. Click the **Replace** tab.
2. Type *Proof* in the **Replace with** field. Review the content to be replaced.
3. Click **Replace** for one instance of the word to be replaced.
4. Click **Replace All** to replace every instance of the word. (There are a total of five instances).
5. Click **close** to close the dialog box when you are finished.
6. **Save** and **close** presentation.

Step 1   Replace Command

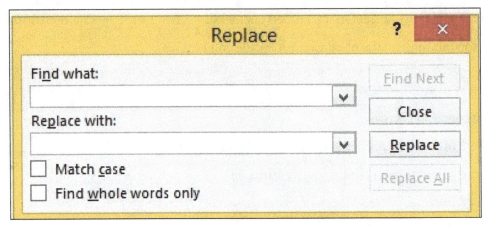

P3.4   Text Alignment and Spacing

The layout of the slide design has preset alignments and text placeholders. The alignment can be modified for vertical or horizontal placement. Text spacing can also be changed so that the text on a slide can be adjusted for more information to be added.

1. Select the **Slide Master** presentation.
2. Select **Slide #1** and select the bulleted text.
3. Choose the **Align Left** command from the **Paragraph** group of the **Home** tab.
4. With the text still selected, pull the down arrow of the **Align Text** command in the **Paragraph** group.
5. Select the **Middle** vertical alignment command.
6. **Save** file.

Step 4 Align Text

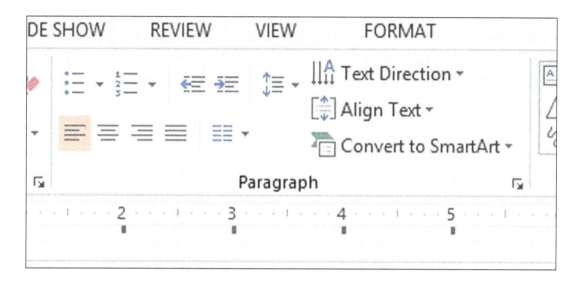

Changing text spacing

1. With **slide master** still open,

2. Select **Slide #2.**

3. Select the bulleted content.

4. On the **Home** tab, select the **paragraph** down-pointing arrow in the far right corner of the **Paragraph** group.

5. Change the **Spacing** in the **Paragraph** dialog box to **before** zero, (0) and **after** zero, (0).

6. Click **OK** when finished. (Notice the **spacing** changed.)

7. **Save** and continue.

P3.4.1 Increasing and Decreasing List Level

Indenting and Aligning Text

1. With **Slide Master** open,

2. Select **Slide #3.**

3. Place the insertion point in front of the second bulleted text (**separate formatting**).

4. From the **Paragraph** group of the **Home** tab, click **Increase List Level**. (**Notice**: the indentation of the text increased one level).

5. Repeat step 4 for the next line.

6. **Save** work and **close.**

Step 4 Increase List Level

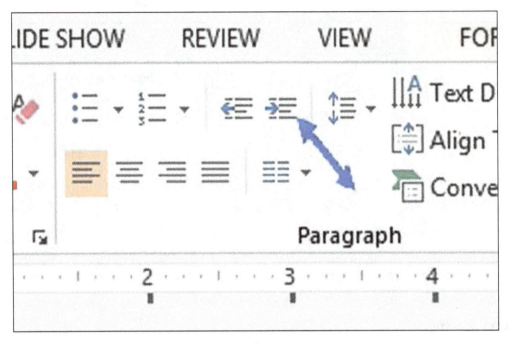

P3.5 Animating Text and Objects

Animation can be used to bring life to your presentation and capture the attention of your audience. **Animation** can be applied to text or objects in your presentation. Animation adds movement to whatever it is applied to.

1. Open the **Applications** presentation.
2. Select **Slide #2** and click the **Animations** tab.
3. Select the bulleted text and pull down the **more** arrow in the **Animation** group.
4. Choose **Wipe** from the **Entrance** animation selection, as shown in Figure 3.1.

   ❖ **Note**: the text box will have a **number** next to it indicating that animation has been applied, as shown in Figure 3.2.
   ❖ A **star** will also appear next to the slide in the **Slide pane** showing that animation has been added to the slide. See Figure 3.3.

5. Repeat step 3 to add animation for slides 3–5 and show a different animation for each slide.
6. **Save** and **close** presentation.

Figure 3.1   Animations

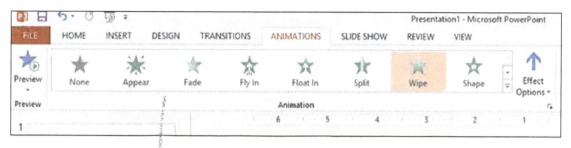

Figure 3.2   Slide with Text Animation

Figure 3.3   Slide Pane View

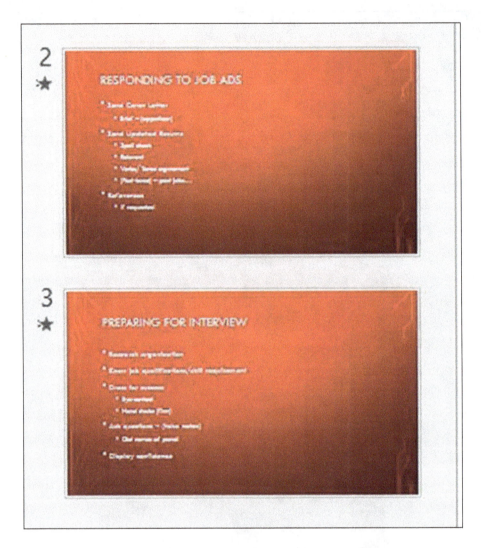

P3.6   Presentation Views

PowerPoint offers different options for viewing your presentation, as shown in Figure 3.4. **Normal** view is for creating slides and editing. **Slide sorter** view allows you to see a thumbnail of the slides with an option to change the slide sequence using the drag and drop feature. **Read mode** shows a maximized preview of the presentation. **Slide show** view is for presenting your presentation to your audience.

A menu will appear in the left corner of the presentation for navigating when you are in **slide show** view. **Notes** page is synonymous with **speaker notes**.

Figure 3.4   Views

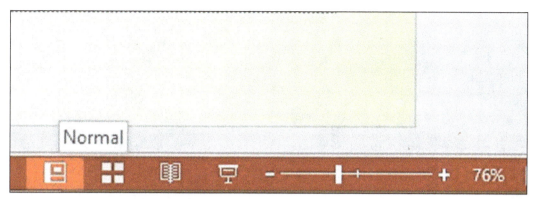

P3.7   Proofing a Presentation—Spell Check

Proofing the presentation is one of the final stages before printing and presenting to your audience. PowerPoint's proofing features assist with checking your presentation for accuracy in grammar and punctuation. Spelling errors are displayed with red **wavy lines** and grammatical errors are displayed with blue **wavy lines**. (See Figure 3.5)

Right click the underlined word and view the suggested spelling or grammar correction. Choose the correct spelling or choose **Ignore** for the line to disappear.

1. Select the **Review** tab.
2. Choose the **Spelling** command in the **Proofing** group.
3. A **Spelling** dialog box opens. See Figure 3.6.
4. The spell checker will highlight words that are not found in the dictionary. You can choose to **ignore** the suggestion or accept the **change**.
5. Click **OK** when **spell check** is completed.

    ❖ The **Options** button backstage will allow you to customize the dictionary and make changes for **proofing** your document.
    ❖ To access **Options**, click the **File** tab.

Figure 3.5   Spelling Error

Step 2   Spelling Command

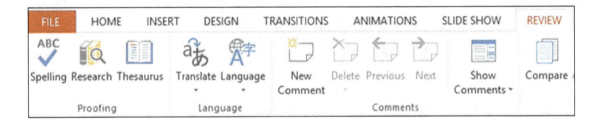

Figure 3.6   Spelling Navigation

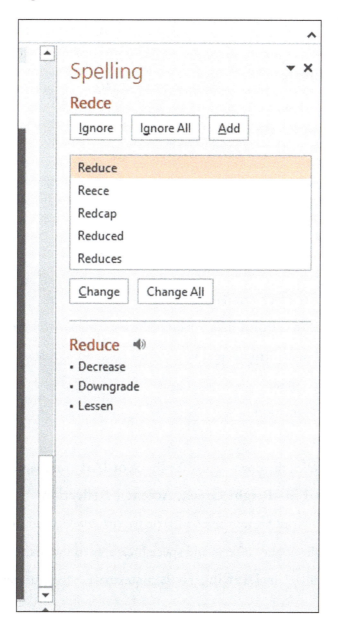

Section 4   Customizing a PowerPoint Presentation

I.   **Inserting WordArt in a Presentation**

II.   **Inserting Shapes**

III.   **Inserting Text Boxes**

IV.   **Inserting SmartArt**

V.   **Inserting Action Buttons**

VI.   **Header/Footer**

VII. **Adding Sound**

VIII. **Formatting Slide Master**

Student Resource Folder—(PowerPoint_P4)

P4.1   Inserting WordArt in a Presentation

WordArt is a feature of **PowerPoint** that enhances the appearance of your presentation. **WordArt** has many styles and effects; it will transform the text in your presentation to make it more vivid and appealing.

1. Open the **Resume** presentation.

2. Select **slide #7**.

3. From the **Insert** tab, click the down arrow for the **WordArt** command in the **Text** group.

4. Choose the **Gradient Fill—Bright Green, Accent 1 Reflection**.

5. Type *Thank you* in the WordArt text box and Type [*your name*] in the subtitle text box. See Figure 4.1.

6. **WordArt** automatically applies effects and special features to the text.

7. Click on the **Format** tab of the **Drawing Tools** contextual tab to adjust or modify the **WordArt** style.

8. **Save** presentation.

Step 3   WordArt Command

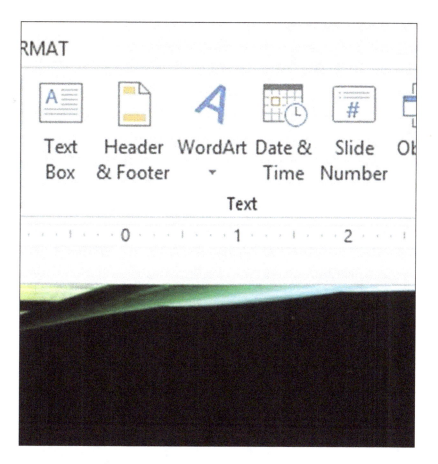

Figure 4.1   Slide Results

P4.2   Inserting Shapes

The **Shapes** command has many features for adding unique visual aid to your presentation and transforming the look of your data.

1. With **Resume** still selected, click the **View** tab and check the box for the **Ruler** in the **show** group.

2. Select **Slide #1.**

3. Click the **Insert** tab. In the **Illustrations** group, pull the down-pointing arrow for the **Shapes** command.

4. Choose the **Left-Right Arrow** from the **Blocked Arrows** category. (Your mouse will appear as a cross.)

5. Position the mouse about one inch under the **title** text box. Left click, and hold to draw **shape**.

6. Click inside **Shape object** (or right click) to insert **text** and type [*Chronological or Functional*], as shown in Figure 4.2.

Step 3   Shapes Command

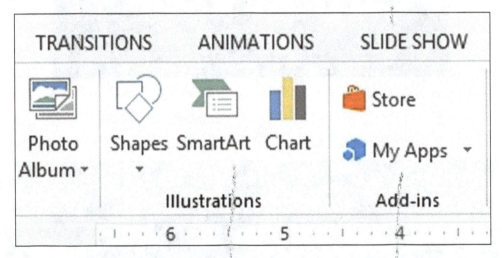

Figure 4.2   Adding Text

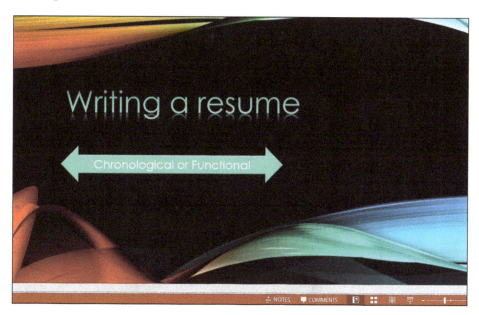

7. With the **Shape** object still selected,

8. Click the **Format** tab from the **Drawing Tools** contextual tab.

9. Click on the **more** down-pointing arrow, in the **Shape Styles** group as, shown in Figure 4.3.

10. Select the Moderate Effect, Bright Green, Accent 5 **shape fill.**

11. **Save** work.

❖ Adjust the height and width of the object with the size handles (**white rectangles**).

❖ Adjust the shape of the object with the **yellow** handles.

❖ Rotate the object with the **rotation** handles.

Figure 4.3   Shapes Styles

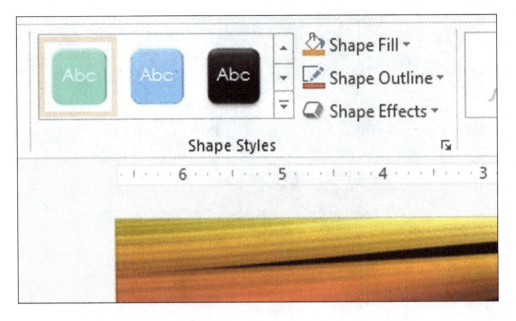

P4.3   Inserting Text Boxes

PowerPoint allows you many options to make adjustments to a presentation by adding additional **text boxes** or other shape objects as needed.

1.   With **resume** still open, making sure the ruler is selected,

2.   Select **Slide #2.**

3.   Click the **Insert** tab and select the **Text Box** command located in the **Text** group. (The mouse appears as a straight down-pointing arrow.)

4.   Click and hold to draw **text** box on the slide.

5.   Draw the **text box** so that the bottom of the **text box** is parallel with the 2-inch mark on the **vertical** ruler and position the end of the **text box** to be parallel with the 5.5-inch mark on the **horizontal** ruler.

6.   With the **text box** still selected type *Employers Want to Know:.* See Figure 4.4.

Figure 4.4   Text Box Modified

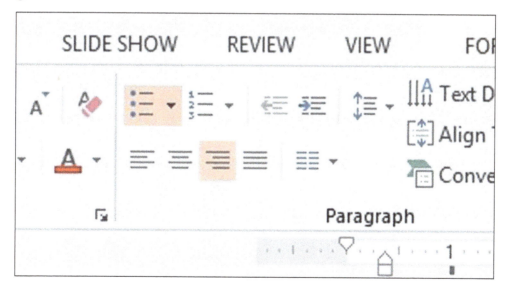

7. Change the **font size**, with text still selected.

8. Select the **Home** tab and select the **Font Size** in the **Font** group. Change the **Font Size** to **48**.

9. Change **alignment**, with text still selected.

10. In the **Paragraph** group of the **Home** tab, select **Align Right**. (Deselect text box when completed.)

11. **Save** work and **close**.

Step 10   Align Text

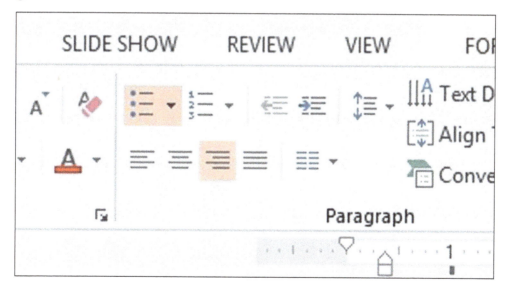

P4.4   Inserting SmartArt into a Presentation

Working with **SmartArt** graphics in a presentation has many advantages. Graphics of any type provide great visual aid for your presentation.

1. Open the **Nutrition** presentation.

2. Select **Slide #2.**

3. Click on the **Insert** tab and select the **SmartArt** command in the **Illustrations** group.

4. From the **Choose a SmartArt Graphic** dialog box, select **Cycle** from the category on the left and choose the **Segmented Cycle** SmartArt.

5. Click **OK**.

Step 4   Choosing SmartArt

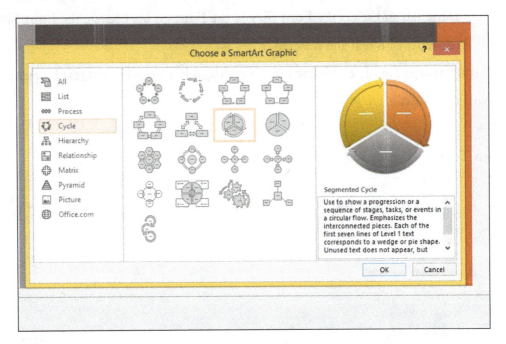

6. Select the **text placeholder** for each food group and type *Fruits, Vegetables, Grains.*

7. With the graphic still selected, click twice to **Add Shape** from the **Design** tab in the **Create Graphic** group of the **SmartArt Tools** contextual tab.

8. Type the remaining food groups: *Protein* and *Dairy*. See Figure 4.5.

9. Click away from the **SmartArt** graphic to deselect it.

Figure 4.5   Modified SmartArt Graphic

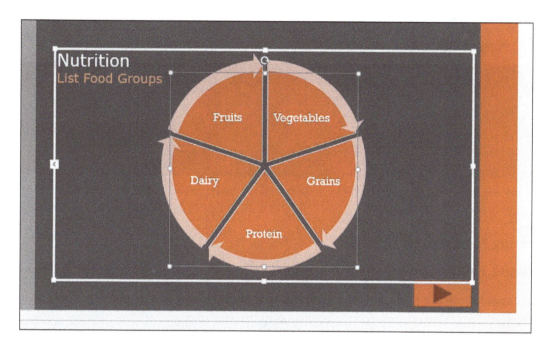

❖ To move the position of a shape, click the move up or down arrow located in the **Design** tab of the **Create Graphic** group.

P4.5   Inserting Action Buttons

PowerPoint has predesigned objects that perform specific tasks that are activated when the presentation is in **Slide Show** view. These predesigned objects are called **Action Buttons**, and they can perform such actions as linking to a particular slide or presentation, linking outside the presentation, or linking to the World Wide Web (WWW).

1. With **Nutrition** still open,

2. Select **Slide #1**.

3. Click the **Insert** tab. Click the down arrow for the **Shapes** command in the **Illustrations** group.

4. Select the **Action Buttons** category (at the bottom) and select the **Action Button, Forward** or **Next.**

5. The mouse now appears like a cross. **Draw** the **action button** in the right corner of the slide.

6. Click **OK** when the **Action Settings** dialog box opens.

7. Repeat step 4–6 for slides 2 and 3.

8. Add the **Home** action button to slides 3 and 8, as shown in Figure 4.6

9. **Save** work.

❖ View **Slide Show** to preview **Action Buttons**

Figure 4.6   Action Buttons

P4.6   Inserting Headers and Footers

Headers and Footers add important information to your document or presentation. Document name, date, and page numbering are just a few of the things that are included in a header and footer.

1. With **Nutrition** still open,

2. Click the **Insert** tab and select the **Header & Footer** command in the **Text** group.

3. Once the **Header & Footer** dialog box opens, click on the **Notes & Handouts** tab.

4. Check the **Date and Time** box, as shown in Figure 4.7.

5. Check the **Header** category and type *Training*.

6. Check the **Footer** category and type [*your last name*].

7. Click **Apply to All**.

8. **Header & Footer** appears in the **Notes & Handouts** of the presentation.

❖ Preview **Notes Page** in the **Presentation Views** group of the **View** tab.

❖ Preview **Handouts** in the **Master Views** group of the **View** tab.

Figure 4.7   Header/Footer

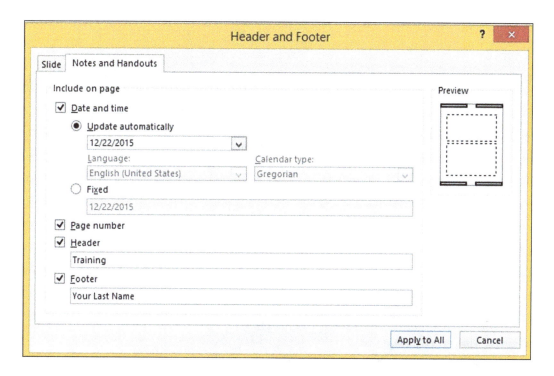

P4.7   Adding Sound

1. With **Nutrition** still open,

2. Select **Slide #8**.

3. Click the **Insert** tab.

4. Select the down arrow for the **Audio** command that is located in the **Media** group.

5. Select the **Audio on My PC**.

6. The **Insert Audio** dialog box opens.

Step 4   Audio Command

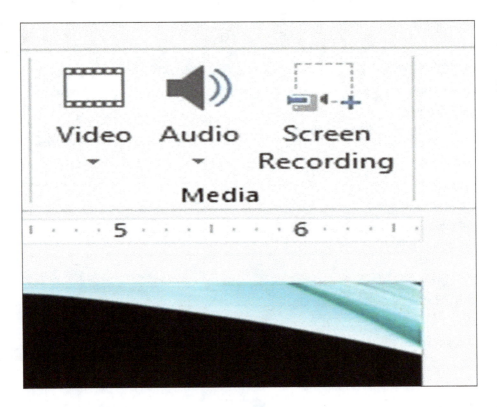

7. Locate your audio file, **Birds101.wav**; **n**otice the Audio Tools contextual tab appears).

8. Select the **Volume** control command from the **Playback** tab under the **Audio Options** group and check **medium** for **volume**.

9. Pull the arrow down for the **Start** command and choose **automatically**.

10. Next, check **Hide During Show**. See Figure 4.8.

11. **Play** sound from the **Preview** group of the **Playback** tab on the **Audio Tools** contextual tabs.

12. Deselect **audio** icon when finished.

13. **Save** and **close**.

Figure 4.8   Voice Control

P4.8   Formatting Slide Master

Each theme in PowerPoint comes with preset formatting. Whenever a slide design is inserted into a presentation, a slide master is also added. Therefore, customizing the **slide master** saves time for modifying each individual slide in the design.

Changes to all slides, background, layout, font formats, design layouts, and placeholders must be done in **Slide Master View**.

1. Open a new, **blank** presentation.
2. Click the **Design** tab and select the **Facet** design from the **Themes group**.
3. Click the **View** tab.
4. Select the **Slide Master** command in the **Master Views** group.
5. Scroll up to the **first** slide to view the **Slide Master**.
6. Select the down arrow for the **colors** command in the **background** group of the **Slide Master** tab as shown in Figure 4.9
7. Select the **Blue Warm** colors from the **Office category**.
8. With the slide master still selected, change the font to **Verdana.**
9. Click to **Close Master View** when finished.
10. **Save** the new design as **My_Facet**. (PowerPoint will save your changes as a customized revision of the design Facet.)

❖ **Hint**: you can also right click the slide and choose **format shape** for other formatting options, as shown in Figure 4.10.

Figure 4.9   Colors Command

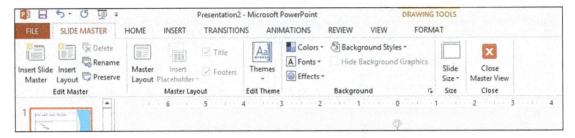

Figure 4.10   Format Shape

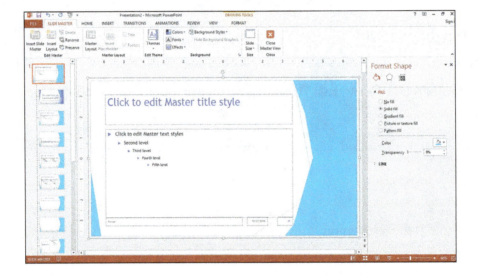

Integrating Other Applications (Word, PowerPoint)

Not only does exporting between PowerPoint and Word provide you with choices for maintaining your document, but exporting can also change the look of your document, thus providing additional choices for viewing and printing.

    I.   **Exporting a PowerPoint Presentation to Word**

   II.   **Exporting a Word Outline to PowerPoint**

Student Resource Files—Int_2

Int-1.1 Exporting PowerPoint to Word

Exporting presentations into a Word document provides another format for viewing PowerPoint handouts and outlines.

1. Open the **WebFiles.pptx** presentation. (Make sure Word is closed.)
2. Click the **file** tab to access **backstage** viewing.
3. Select the **exports** tab and choose the **create handouts** command.
4. Under the **Create Handouts in Microsoft Word** section, (on the right) click **create handouts**. (Notice the **Send to Microsoft Word** dialog box opens).
5. Select **blank lines next to slides**.
6. Click **OK**. (PowerPoint will automatically create and display the handouts in Word).
7. **Save** the file as **My_WebFiles.docx** and **close** the document.

Step 4 **Create Handouts**

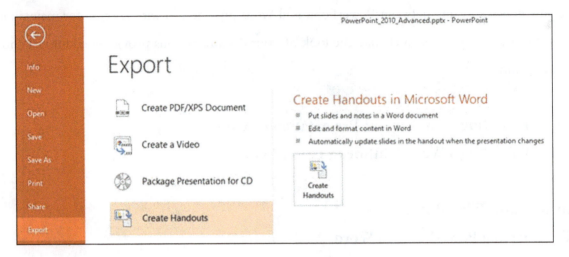

Step 5 **Word Layout Features**

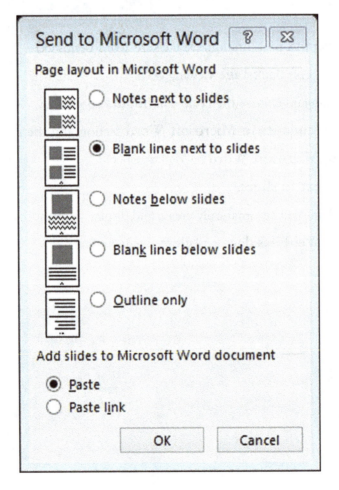

Int-1.2 Exporting a Word Outline to PowerPoint

Follow the steps below to make sure the **Send to Microsoft PowerPoint** command is on the Quick Access Toolbar for this exercise.

1. Open the **Outline** document.

2. Click the file tab and select options.

3. Select the Quick Access Toolbar command.

4. Under the **Choose commands from** category on the left, select **all commands** from the drop-down arrow, as shown in Figure 1.

5. Select **Send to Microsoft PowerPoint** from the list.

6. Select **add** to move the command to the right column under **customizing quick access toolbar.**

7. Click **OK**. The new button now appears on the Quick Access Toolbar.

8. Select the **Send to Microsoft PowerPoint** command from the Quick Access Toolbar.

9. View how PowerPoint separates each Header Style in the PowerPoint slides. Compare how each bulleted text is separated on different slides. Heading Styles will help to change the look of your document, and it will also change the layout of your presentation outline.

10. Save PowerPoint as **My_Outline**

11. **Close** document when finished.

Figure 1   Send to Microsoft PowerPoint Command

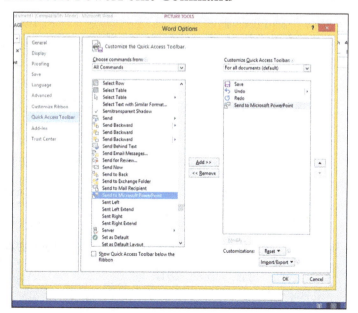

Index

PowerPoint 2013

Knowledge and Skill Assessment

P1   Knowledge Check

1.   Which tab gives you access to **backstage** viewing? _____

2.   The undo command is located on the _____ _____ toolbar.

3.   The **ribbon** consists of **tabs** and _____.

4.   Predesigned PowerPoint presentations are called _____.

5.   Customize **tabs** and **groups** can be added through the **Options** command by accessing the _____tab.

6.   The _____ _____ _____command will **Hide/Show** the **Ribbon**.

7.   Click the _____command to search file formats for **audio** that may be used in PowerPoint.

P2   Knowledge Check

1.   Access the _____ _____ to view previously saved files on your computer.

2.   To insert a **new slide**, click the _____ _____command.

3.   **Transitions** can be added to a slide by clicking the _____tab.

4.   There are _____categories of **transitions**.

5.   _____themes can be modified to bring a consistent look to a presentation.

6.   Select the _____ tab to run a presentation from the **Ribbon**.

7.   The _____ option saves the presentation on the **Quick Access Toolbar**.

P3   Knowledge Check

1.   Click the _____tab to access the **Spelling** command for document proofing.

2.   After accessing the **Options** button; click the _____tab to **customize the dictionary** in Word.

3.   The _____ category is where you choose the animation for objects exiting a slide.

4.   **Increasing the list level** moves text to the _____ of the slide.

5.   To apply **before and after spacing** in a paragraph, access the **paragraph** command in the _____group.

6.   Click the _____ _____ command to **vertically align** text on the page.

7.   Click the _____command to **Find/Replace** text in a document.

P4   Knowledge Check

1. **Action Buttons** are located in the _____group of the **Insert** tab.

2. The _____ and _____category is where the **five-point star** is located.

3. With the star selected, the _____ _____ contextual tab appears; and any changes to the object's **shape** and style can be made with the _____ tab selected.

4. Click inside the **text box** to add text. True/False

5. Once the **Header/Footer** is applied to the **slide** tab, it is automatically applied to the **Notes & Handout** tab. True/False

6. Click the _____tab to view the **Notes Page** in the **Presentation Views** group.

7. To make changes to all slides in the Design Themes layout, select the _____ _____.

Skill Assessments 1 and 2

(Insert a Template, Insert WordArt, Insert Shape, and Apply Transition)

1. Modify a presentation for **Dynasties Inc**.

2. From the **suggested searches** topic selections, choose **Orientation** and select **Employee Orientation**. (**Note**: See student resource folder if you are unable to locate the suggested topic selection.)

3. Select **Slide #1**. Replace subtitle text [**Your Company Name and Logo**] with [**Dynasties Inc.**]

4. Make sure subtitle is selected and click on the **Format** tab of the **Drawing Tools** contextual tab.

5. Select the **more** drop-down command in the **WordArt Styles** group.

6. Choose **Fill-Dark Red, Accent 1, Shadow.**

7. Insert a **5-Point Star** in the bottom right corner of the slide and repeat step 6 if color does not fill automatically.

8. Change the subtitle font size to [**22**].

9. Change the **Design theme** to [**Ion**].

10. Add the **Shape** Transition to slides 1–4.

11. **Delete** slide #9 and replace it with a new Title Slide. Type *Thank you* in the title placeholder.

12. Horizontally **center** the text [**Thank-you**] and align vertically to the **middle**.

13. **Run** the presentation.

14. **Save** the presentation as **DynastiesInc.**

15. **Close.**

Skill Assessment 3

(Modify a Presentation, Apply Transition and Animation)

Student Resource Folder—(SkillAssessment_P3)

1. Open the **ZFitness** presentation.
2. Select **slide #3.**
3. Change the **Font** to Calibri (Body) and change the **Font size** to 24.
4. Select **slide #7** and **cut** the last three bullets from the slide beginning with, [**Water . . ., Towel . . ., $5-$10 . . .**].
5. Select **slide #6** and **paste** the cut text. (Adjust the text box if needed.)
6. Select **slide #9** and change the list levels for [**cross trainers, dance,** and **running**] to match the list level of [**dance movements**].
7. Spell check the document. (**Note**: frustrated is spelled incorrectly; accept the change and close the navigation pane).
8. **Find** Zumba and **replace** with Zumba Fitness. (Replace all except the title slide on slide #1).
9. **Animate** text on **slide #10** with **wipe** animation.
10. Add **wipe transition** to **slide #1**.
11. **Run** the presentation.
12. **Save** and close.

Skill Assessment 4

(Modify a Presentation, Format Slide Master, Insert SmartArt, WordArt, Apply Transition, Animation, and Insert Sound to a Slide)

Student Resource Folder—(SkillAssessment_P4)

1. Open the **SC_Attractions** presentation.
2. Format the **Slide Master** with the following:
   a. Format shape, add a shape **solid fill** color—Blue Accent 1.
   b. Add a **solid line** color—Dark Blue.
3. Modify **slide #1** of the presentation with the following:
   a. Delete the title text box and replace it with **WordArt.**

b. Type **[Tourist Attractions]** for the new title and choose Fill-Blue, Accent 1, Shadow.

c. Vertically align text box with the subtitle text box.

d. Align text right.

e. Change the font size to 60.

f. Apply **Text Outline**—Dark Blue.

4. Insert four Title and Content Slides into the presentation. Type data for slides 2–4, as shown below.

5. Choose the **Continuous block process,** SmartArt graphic for **slide #5**. (Add data to SmartArt, as shown below.)

6. **Animate** SmartArt

   a. Apply **wheel entrance**

   b. Add **effect options**

      i. Apply 8 **spokes**

      ii. **Sequence** one-by-one

7. Add split **transition** to slides 1–3.

8. Insert **header/footer** data in the **notes and handouts** tab.

9. Insert next **action buttons** on slides 1–5.

10. Add **sound** of your preference to **slide #1**.

11. **Save** and **close** presentation.

Slide 2

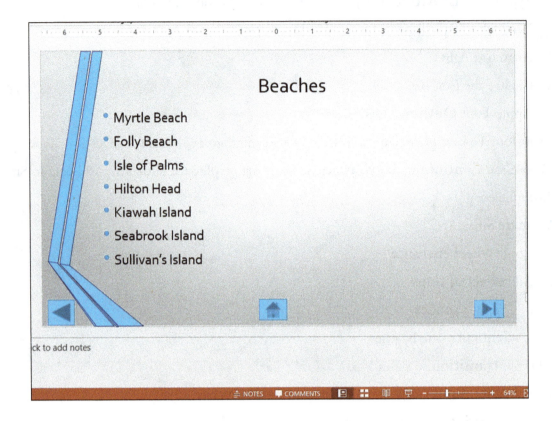

Slide 3

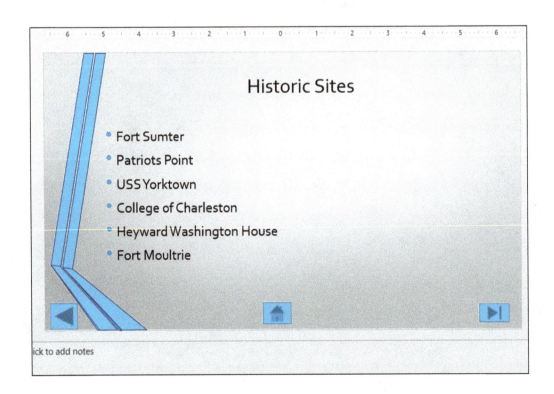

Slide 4

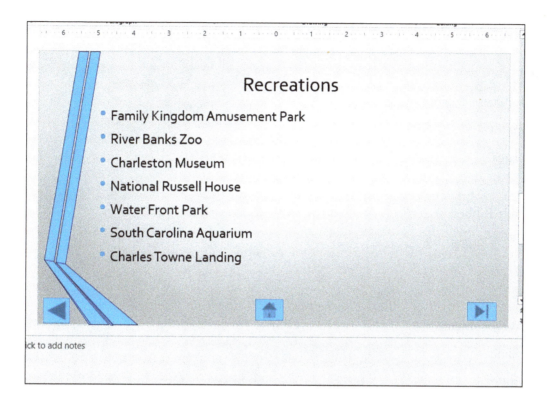

Slide 5 (SmartArt]

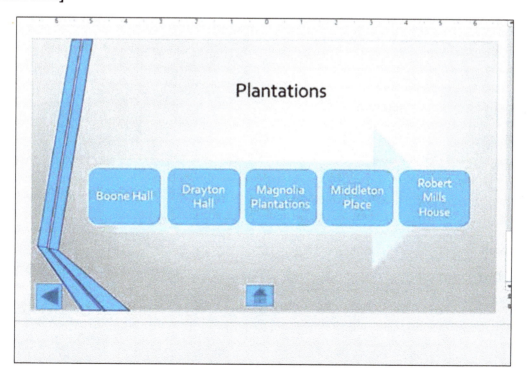

Knowledge Check Answers

Answers P1

1. File
2. Quick Access Toolbar
3. Groups
4. Templates
5. File
6. Autohide Ribbon
7. **Help**

Answers P2

1. Recent Documents
2. New Slide
3. Transition
4. Three
5. Design
6. Slide Show
7. Save

Answers P3

1. Review
2. Proofing
3. Exit
4. Right
5. Paragraph
6. Align Text
7. Find

Answers P4

1. Illustrations

2. Stars and Banners

3. Drawing tools, Format

4. True

5. False

6. View

7. Slide Master